GARDEN

EVOLUTION OF

OF ENGLAND

HISTORIC GARDENS IN

KENT

ELISABETH HALL

In association with Kent County Council
and the Kent Gardens Trust.

THE GARDEN OF ENGLAND
CONTENTS:

Introduction – The Garden of England 3-4

Chapter I – Special features 5-13

Chapter 2 – Mediaeval into Tudor 14-15

Chapter 3 – Hints of Italy 16-21

Chapter 4 – The formal French and Dutch styles 22-27

Chapter 5 – The Landscape Garden 28-35

Chapter 6 – Diversity in the 19th century 36-43

Chapter 7 – The 20th century 44-49

Chapter 8 – The Plantsman's garden 50-55

Chapter 9 – Conservation and Restoration 56-62

Gazeteer 63-70

Bibliography 71

Acknowledgements 71

Index 72

Topiary at Chilham

❧ THE GARDEN OF ENGLAND ❧

By Elisabeth Hall ~ Historian to The Kent Gardens Trust

Kent has long been known as the 'Garden of England', a title still fully deserved today. Industrialisation has been largely confined to north west Kent and the Medway Valley, and though urbanisation has spread on the London fringe, the strong tradition of gardening in the county has ameliorated these intrusions. There are more gardens open to the public here than in any other county, (179 in 1994), horticultural societies abound and the acreage of the orchards that one suspects originally earned Kent its title, is still much the highest of any county in the United Kingdom, with 13,430 hectares of top fruit and 271 hectares of small fruit and vines. These special features excite the curiosity, giving impetus for an interpretation of their development.

It is hoped that a better understanding of these special qualities of Kent's gardens can be achieved by studying a selected group in the context of changing fashions in garden design through the ages. In this way a visitor's enjoyment and appreciation of surviving individual gardens and parks can also be much enhanced.

Historical evidence of past garden styles is abundant, although of Roman gardens little tangible has been discovered in Kent. **Fishbourne Palace** Gardens in Sussex however, is a scholarly recreation based upon excellent archaeological evidence. Man's struggle to tame nature in mediaeval times can be more easily traced where the enclosing walls remain. Such survive at **Canterbury Cathedral** and the **Archbishop's Palace**, Maidstone. Contemporary illustrations tell us of rectangular beds filled with vegetables, herbs and flowers. The late mediaeval fashion for mounts brought the outside world into view, perhaps an orchard or deer park, or from Tudor times, the knot garden.

In the Tudor period the influence of the Italian renaissance garden had a particularly strong impact in Kent. Many garden contours were reworked into terraces, and water gardens became significant and elaborate features. The latter often incorporated former moats, while the castle turret principle was used in the gazebos placed on the highest terrace, as an eyecatching alternative to the mount. As in Italy, sculpture was prominent. Gardens incorporating such features can still be seen at **Penshurst Place, Knole, Northbourne Court, Hales Place, Groombridge, Ightham Mote** and **Roydon Hall** - a fascinating group.

The creation of the great formal garden at Versailles from the 1660s was to give rise to similar ambitions in England, albeit on a smaller scale, thus extending formality beyond the walled garden through patterns of avenues and 'outdoor rooms' between trees. The French style was, not surprisingly, well represented in Kent, judging both by present day remains and documentation. **Squerryes** at Westerham is a well documented example. However, by the 1720s a reaction against formality was gathering strength, and man's control over nature had become such that he encouraged its imitation in its most idealised, painterly form, to embrace his whole estate. Thus was born the English Landscape Garden. This fashion was to prove less appropriate for Kent because of the county's relatively dense population. The chief practitioner, **'Capability' Brown** (1715-83) gained few commissions here, and these were small in scale.

Stoneacre, Otham.

still put into practice today. Robinson promoted a wilder more natural kind of plantsman's garden, no doubt stimulated by the great influx of new plants to Britain from all over the world. Jekyll contributed an artist's eye, with its emphasis on coordination of colour and texture. Thus was born the **Arts and Crafts Garden**, still favoured by Kent's gardeners, most appropriately when ornamenting the grounds of former ancient yeoman's houses as at **Stoneacre** or romantic castle remains as at **Sissinghurst!**

Recent years have seen a greater public awareness of the need to conserve these ephemeral, yet characteristically British creations. For example, there have been the setting up of adult education classes in garden history and the growth of the county garden trust movement. The analysis that follows has been carried out as a result of such stimulating developments. Indeed the **Kent Gardens Trust** has supported the publication of this volume, which the author hopes will assist in their work of garden restoration, and also indicate areas for future research.

Humphry Repton (1752-1818) fared much better, for from 1790 he was taken up by villa builder and aristocrat alike. His more picturesque version of the landscape garden including ornamentation of the areas near the house, as at **Cobham Hall** near Rochester, remained long in favour. By the 1840's a more flamboyant, in some ways more artificial, Franco-Italian formal style was reasserting itself, through its leading exponent, **William Andrews Nesfield** (1793-1881), well known for his landscaping at **Regent's Park, Kew Gardens** and the **Royal Horticultural Society gardens in Kensington**. Of his many commissions in Kent, **Oxonhoath**, near Hadlow is by far the least altered. Italian themes continued to influence design into the present century, **Hever Castle garden** being a glamorous example.

Astonishingly, it has been the concepts of the author and publisher, **William Robinson** (1838-1935), and of **Gertrude Jekyll** (1843-1932) that have proved to form the longest lasting of trends. For their ideas, vigorously expounded first in the 1870s, are

Oxonhoath flower fountain c1845-46

CHAPTER 1

❧ SPECIAL FEATURES ❧

F actors that have made an impact on the individuality of the historic gardens of Kent include the climate and geology, the wide range of plant material flourishing in the county and the many distinguished gardeners, writers and designers who have worked there.

Plant material

The outstanding quality of Kent gardens undoubtedly lies largely in the extraordinary variety of plants that will grow successfully there. Added to this, throughout the present century there have developed a large number of specialist nurseries and amateur gardeners and their concomitant societies, whose combined knowledge makes maximum use of this special facility. Kent's gardeners also played a prominent and productive part in world wide plant hunting expeditions, to the benefit of their own and The Nation's gardens.

The indigenous common oak however, still predominates as a specimen tree in most parkland landscapes, while many a long lived sweet chestnut or lime avenue survives to indicate their popularity for such use since the 17th century. Evergreen oaks, introduced from the Mediterranean, are particularly abundant in East Kent coast parks such as **Knowlton** and **Quex**, whether for wind protection or year round colour and massing.

Orchards fulfilled an even more important dual role before the influx of foreign imports in the later 19th century. Kent's supremacy in fruit growing was described by **Lambarde** in his *Perambulations* of 1571:

'but as for orchards of apples and gardens of cherries, and those of the most delicious and exquisite kinds that can be, no part of the realme (that I know) hath them either in such quantity and number, or with such arte and industrie set and planted.'

The earliest illustrations show garden walls espaliered or cordoned; and orchards were brought very close to the house. This state still apertains at **Penshurst**, where they were planting yellow peaches and apricots *'against the church wall, which faces east'* as early as 1595, and where the diarist **Samuel Pepys**, once admired the fruit blossom.

Nurserymen's bills for flowers at Penshurst a few years later, indicate that native plants were still popular. Purchases in April 1633 included four and a half dozen primroses, twelve dozen violets –also doubles– one dozen pansies, cowslips, oxlips, roses and some wallflowers. At the same time a few exotics including some from eastern North America and the West Indies, were being given publicity in the first florist's books, **John Parkinson's** *Paradisus* (1629), and his *Theatrum botanicum* (1640). They included the runner bean (then grown ornamentally), Virginia creeper and black Virginian walnut. The false acacia or Robinia, which has long been a popular ornamental tree in Kent, (perhaps the oldest of them now being that at **Cobham Court**, Bekesbourne), is mentioned as growing in the **Tradescants' garden** in **Lambeth** 1634. In the late 17th and throughout the 18th century, conifers, deciduous trees and flowering shrubs from eastern North America continued to be introduced and were avidly collected. A plan for the garden at Cobham near Rochester, of 1789, for example shows a long terrace bed labelled simply 'America'. An account from the nurseryman Lewis Kennedy for the **Earl of Stanhope's** garden at **Chevening**, has among American plants : 2 *liquidambers* at 4/- each, a *catalpa* at 2/- a trumpet flower (*Campsis radicans*) at 2/-, 2 scarlet oaks at 5/- and 2 Newfoundland dogwood at 1/-. Violets are again included and double primroses quoted as 'omitted' from the order.

These early trees brought from the British colonies have not proved long lived enough for an assessment of their impact to be made. On the other hand conifers, such as Douglas Fir and Wellingtonia, introduced from the western coast of America in 1823 and 1853 respectively, and the Atlantic Blue Cedar from Morocco in the 1840s, still abound from

A fine ginko in Cobham Hall Irregular Flower Garden.

original plantings and often form indicators for additional 19th century activity in otherwise 18th century landscape parks. Some of the finest 19th century exotic tree plantings, though all much ravaged in the gale of 1987, occur at **Leigh Place,** near Penshurst, **Cobham Hall**, near Rochester and **Linton Park**, near Maidstone. At Cobham are two splendid *Gingko biloba* or Maidenhair Trees**,** one of the first species to be introduced from China in the mid 18th century.

By the end of the 19th century the fashionable woodland gardens became a treasury for the newly introduced Chinese, Japanese and Himalayan trees and flowering shrubs. They included the Deodar cedar, species *rhododendron, azalea, magnolia, camellia* and *Davidia involucrata* or Handkerchief Tree, which

men such as **Robert Fortune**, **Abbé Armand David** and **Augustine Henry** had brought to Europe. In the early 20th century **E.H.Wilson** augmented this supply most notably, especially with his introduction of the *Lilium regale* from a remote Chinese valley. For a county once famous for cherry orchards it seems appropriate that one of the chief glories of its 20th century gardens is the many varieties of the ornamental cherry, introduced from Japan by **Captain Collingwood Ingram** of **Benenden Grange** (now Collingwood Grange). For all these exotic plants Kent probably has the most advantageous conditions, as species considered half hardy elsewhere often survive here in the winter: always an astonishment to visitors is the Chusan palm in the close at Rochester Cathedral. The record is equally good for normally tender evergreens, which survive all but the worst winters. For example the bay and myrtle flourish as well as the more recently introduced *Ceanothus* evergreen varieties, several *Olearia* (the daisy bushes of New Zealand), and the exotic *Crinodendron hookerianum* with its red bell flowers. Of wall plants one may name the Banksian rose, *Azara microphylla* and *Cytisus battandieri* - all shades of yellow. Alpines, which became popular from the mid 19th century, flourish on the chalk and sandy soils in the abundant sunshine and were extensively planted in the many artificial rock or 'Pulhamite' rock gardens so freely created toward the end of the 19th century, particularly at seaside resorts.

As elsewhere in the country, the peak period for growing tender plants was from the middle of the 19th century to the outbreak of the Great War in 1914. As well as the addition of conservatories adjacent to the house, much glass was added to kitchen gardens. Some larger estates developed specialised greenhouse gardens, like the one surviving at **Quex Park** - the remnants of an even more elaborate complex survives at David Salomon's house, Broom Hill, Southborough.

The famous Japanese Kanzan cherry.

Records from **Linton Park** of 1844 list tender exotics obtained 'at trade' for growing in their greenhouses, a number of them tropical orchid species. The Head Gardener, **Mr John Robson** kept a diary, which in 1864 described the specialist use of each greenhouse for vines, peaches, orchids, ferns, and plants for the house, a pattern of luxury that was to become typical. Particularly famous in the second half of the century were the winter gardens at **Avery Hill Park, Eltham**, with cold, temperate and tropical houses.

Throughout the last two hundred years, gardeners seem to have soaked up new varieties and species like a sponge and this trend continues apace. Nurserymen introducing new or perhaps long lost plants to cultivation have the added stimulus of a vigorous **Hardy Plant Society** and the **National Council for the Conservation of Plants and Gardens (N.C.C.P.G).** At their plant sales, specialist nurseries and the multitude of gifted amateurs exchange their treasures. Some garden centres quickly take up the new challenges too. Here perhaps the hope for the future, at a time when training opportunities for budding professional gardeners are ever diminishing.

Geology and climate

The special popularity of gardening in Kent must be connected to the climate, which most nearly approaches that of mainland Europe, being warmer and dryer and with higher sunshine levels than in most of England. This gives considerable advantage, particularly in the growing of half hardy and difficult plants, for seed development and the growth of self sown seedlings.

Furthermore, the considerable variety of rocks and soils give the widest possible range of growing conditions.

The chalk Downs of North and East Kent are ideal for alkaline loving plants, while the High and Low Weald encourage acid lovers such as

Quex Park. Former glasshouse garden (Picture taken circa 1990). Walls late Georgian.

rhododendrons and azaleas. The latter form the dominant spring feature of many woodland gardens, some of the finest of which are situated along the greensand ridge partly encircling Kent and Sussex. **Wakehurst**, **Leonardslee** and **Nymans** are on the southern ridge, **Chartwell** and **Emmetts** on the

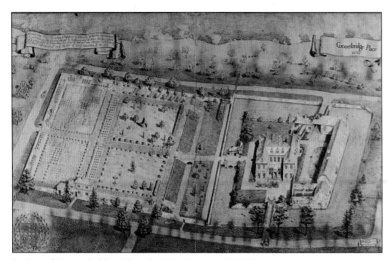

A plan of Groombridge Place by C.E. Kempe. (1884)

northern one. Other gardens flourish on Wealden clays. Examples include **Scotney Castle, Hole Park** and **Pympne Manor**, with their 'Himalayan valley' gardens, glorious in spring when rhododendrons, azaleas and other exotics bloom. The most famous of all, **Sissinghurst Castle**, also lies in the Weald. The rich alluvial soils that cover parts of the Weald and the north Kent chalk belt, as well as the benevolent climate, are factors particularly benefitting fruit growing.

The siting and design of some of the finest gardens have been affected by the often dramatic changes of level. The greensand ridge south of the northern chalk Downs allows panoramic views across the Weald. These prospects seem to have been consciously utilised since the late 18th century, as at **Linton, Riverhill, Oxonhoath** and **Boughton Place**, though in the latter two cases the mansions themselves are much earlier. A traveller down the M25 between Wrotham and Westerham will see many a large Edwardian villa garden sited on the chalk ridge overlooking the Weald. A lesser ridge is formed by the rocks of the High Weald in the Tunbridge Wells area, giving extensive vistas from the 19th century villa gardens on the south side of the Pembury Road, **Dunorlan** being an especially notable example. The rocks themselves were considered a novelty in the 17th century **High Rocks Park**, Tunbridge Wells, perhaps one of the earliest 'rock' gardens in Britain. The latter is an honour more often given to **Redleaf** near Penshurst, a lively, original creation of the 1820s, by an ancestor of **H.G. Wells**, using a quarry already on the site. The Penshurst rock also formed the basis for perhaps the most dramatic rock garden of all, **Swaylands**, formed at the end of the 19th century, in part under the ownership of **George Drummond** the banker.

Down in the valleys, especially those in the lee of the High Weald ridge, villages flourished on account of their iron and wool industries. Their older manor houses, or yeoman's farm houses, have in time become the focus of historic gardens. **Groombridge Place** is one such, dramatically sited in a steep sided valley and still surrounded by its moat. Here the present garden was laid out in the 17th century. **Penshurst Place**, within its ancient deer park, is the earliest well documented garden in Kent, begun before 1567. The views from the terraces extend over the broad Wealden valley. **Marle Place** and **Crittenden** have 20th century gardens, similarly sheltered, ornamenting their former yeoman's farms.

At Crittenden the hammer pond is an important focus, an ingenious reuse of a former industrial site. Probably the grandest example of the use of such industrial relics is the great Sussex garden of **Leonardslee**. Water, as a feature, as well as for more practical purposes, is a scarce resource in Kent. **Humphry Repton**, working at **Cobham** in 1791, noted the lack of it on the chalk and rather facetiously

Garden Sites and Geology

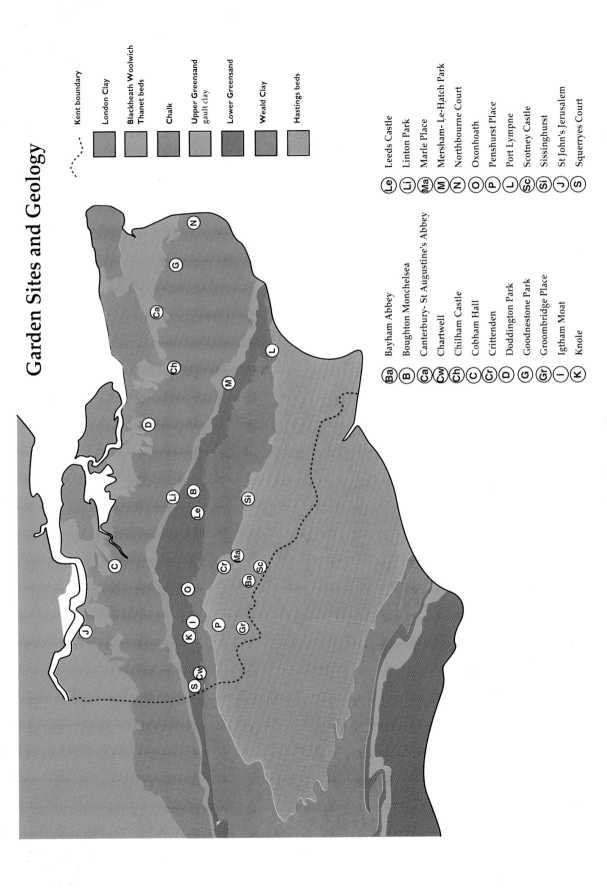

Kent boundary

London Clay

Blackheath Woolwich
Thanet beds

Chalk

Upper Greensand
gault clay

Lower Greensand

Weald Clay

Hastings beds

(Ba) Bayham Abbey
(B) Boughton Monchelsea
(Ca) Canterbury- St Augustine's Abbey
(Cw) Chartwell
(Ch) Chilham Castle
(C) Cobham Hall
(Cr) Crittenden
(D) Doddington Park
(G) Goodnestone Park
(Gr) Groombridge Place
(I) Igtham Moat
(K) Knole

(Le) Leeds Castle
(Li) Linton Park
(Ma) Marle Place
(M) Mersham- Le-Hatch Park
(N) Northbourne Court
(O) Oxonhoath
(P) Penshurst Place
(L) Port Lympne
(Sc) Scotney Castle
(Si) Sissinghurst
(J) St John's Jerusalem
(S) Squerryes Court

suggested that the Elizabethan great house perfectly ornamented precisely that situation in the park where the lake should be. The many estates around the Nailbourne Valley in north-east Kent can hardly rely on the fitful Nailbourne rivulet. However landscape parks south of the chalk downs are better favoured. At **Chevening, Squerryes, Leeds Castle** and the 20th century **Port Lympne**, water forms the essential focus, while at **Mersham -le-Hatch** the former fish ponds add reflection and sparkle to the view of the great east facade from the Stour valley.

Famous gardeners and garden writers

The famous royal gardeners, the **Tradescants**, father and son, both have strong connections with Kent, particularly the father, John sen.(circa1570 - 1638), who married a Meopham girl and worked for **Lord Wotton** at **St. Augustine's,** Canterbury, and with **Sir Dudley Digges** of Chilham. He sent his son, John (1608-1662) to the King's School at Canterbury.

Mersham-le-Hatch, House from lake.

The two men were the first professional plant hunters, the elder in the Old World, the younger in the new colony of Virginia. They recorded the contents of their famous garden at Lambeth, which contained many of their new introductions, such as the *Robinia pseudoacacia*, which flourishes in the county. An important byproduct of their expeditions were inanimate 'curiosities' which were also on display to the public at Lambeth, in the 'Ark'. It can fairly be said that the whole collection, the *'Museum Tradescantorum'* became the foundation for the public museum movement in England.

Contemporary with these innovators, was **Thomas Johnson** (d. 1644), apothecary, who wrote the foreword to the second edition of **Gerard's** *Herbal* in 1622. He also recorded some of the botanical finds in the Kent countryside-the first of such records. More specifically horticultural, were the writings of **John Evelyn** (1620-1676), the great promoter of forestry. His handsome and fashionable Italianate garden at **Sayes Court**, Deptford, was renowned and he visited and recorded other significant Kent gardens. His book, *Sylva* (1664) was very influential in promoting tree plantations as new gardens were created in the following century.

The brothers **Sherard-James** (1666-1738) and **William** (1659-1758), followed in the Evelyn tradition of combining garden creation with a keen botanical interest. They were also avid plant collectors in Europe. The notable contents of their garden at Eltham were published by **J.J.Dillenius** with finely engraved illustrations in two volumes - *Hortus Elthamensis* (1733), one of the first such publications in England.

Of the many 18th century improvers of their estates, the **Knatchbulls** of **Mersham-le-Hatch** were followers of Evelyn in their enthusiasm for tree plantations. A map of 1747 shows specific wildernesses for firs and chestnuts. They were also enthusiastic planters of exotics, and **Wyndham Knatchbull** described other well known gardens in his diary.

Lively vignettes of Victorian gardening have been left by some prominent practical gardeners. For Linton Park there are the carefully kept diaries of **John Robson,** the head gardener from circa 1849-76. He also wrote extensively about other gardens in the horticultural magazines of the day, which contain splendid resource material for many Victorian gardens. Near by at Maidstone, **George Bunyard** (1841-1919), an outstanding representative of the family firm of fruit growers and general nurserymen, was also a horticultural writer,

Dean Hole's garden at the Deanery, Rochester painted by George Elgood (circa 1900)

specialising in books on fruit cultivation. In 1880, at the peak of his career, his nursery had three hundred acres of fruit trees and fifty glasshouses. He was able to make a presentation of 125 dishes of fruit at the Royal Horticultural Society, which won a gold medal.

The English tradition of amateurism thrived in the person of **Dean Samuel Reynolds Hole** (1819-1904) who became dean of Rochester Cathedral in 1887, and who had previously made his name as a rosarian and author. Becoming curate and vicar at Caunton, Lincs, Hole cultivated roses in his large garden, at a period when the great number of new varieties being produced made rose growing extremely popular. His enthusiasm brought about the first Grand National Rose show in 1858 and the foundation of the **National Rose Society**. He was author of several gardening books of a didactic kind. Hole's *Book about Roses* came out in 1869 and ran to over twenty editions.

Captain Collingwood Ingram (1882-1983) was both plant hunter and gardener, and left journals and papers which have not yet been fully published. His introduction of many of the Japanese ornamental cherry varieties has made a rich contribution to horticulture and revolutionised roadside planting.

Ingram cultivated these together with many other new species and specialities in his garden at **Benenden Grange**. Plans are afoot at the time of writing, to restore his woodland garden.

A plantswoman of a different ilk, **Vita Sackville-West** (1892-1962), daughter of the 3rd Baron Sackville of Knole and wife of the writer, **Harold Nicholson**, has become something of a legend. In the twenties she made a distinguished reputation as a writer and poet. Together with Harold Nicholson she found her métier as a garden designer and plantswoman creating a new garden at their first family home, **Hall Barn**, near Sevenoaks, and soon after, and most memorably, at **Sissinghurst**. She shared her gardening experiences with the general public in her long series of elegant and evocative articles in **The Observer**.

The outstanding popularity of Sissinghurst Castle gardens forms a continuing testimony to the genius of the partnership between Vita and her husband.

Of the 20th century practitioners in a grander manner, **Philip Tilden** (1887-1956) has left his mark in

Lilium auratum at Sissinghurst Castle

Kent, most impressively at **Port Lympne**, working for Sir Philip Sassoon. He also made a garden at **Allington Castle**, but is probably best known for his landscaping of the grounds at **Chartwell** for **Sir Winston Churchill.**

ST. AUGUSTINE'S ABBEY
CANTERBURY 1642

1. mount
2. bason
3. island
4. Charon in boat with spouting creatures
5. watery nymphs
6. knot garden
7. lime tree walk
8. orchard
9. Abbey
10. wall

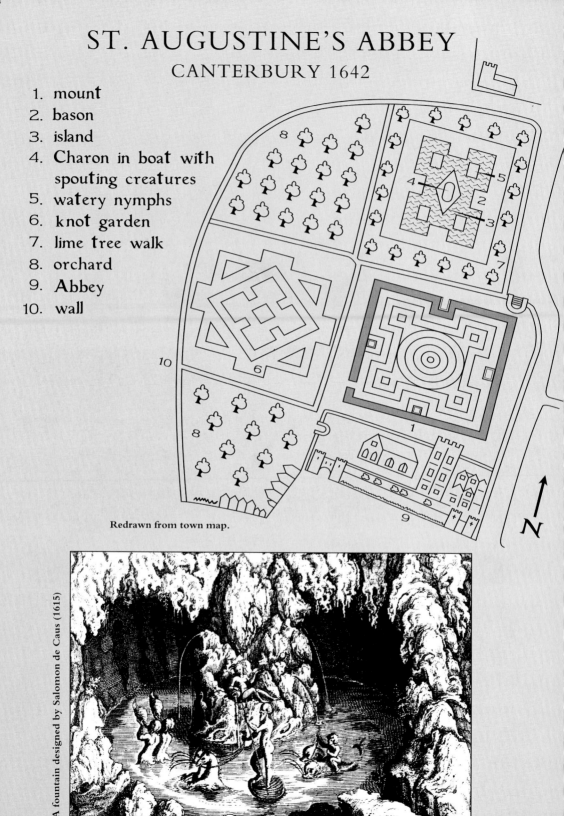

Redrawn from town map.

A fountain designed by Salomon de Caus (1615)

Part of the terraces at Chilham Castle (17th – 20th Century)

CHAPTER 2

❧MEDIAEVAL INTO TUDOR❧

I t is impossible to understand fully any individual garden in Kent without appreciating how its present layout and appearance have been altered by a continuous process of historical change, resulting quite often in a mosaic of designs even where one theme is dominant. The following chapters will outline the main styles and discuss these with reference to specific sites. In addition each chapter will focus upon a particular garden as a representative 'case-study'.

Our knowledge of mediaeval gardens depends largely on written sources. The Tudor historian **Lambarde** listed 55 mediaeval deer parks and forests in Kent, though many of them have since been disparked. They were enclosed by steep banks surmounted by a park pale fence. Under the severe contemporary game laws the establishment of each deer park needed the permission of the king. These

The deer park at Knole

hunting domains, together with the manors with which they were connected, still form the basis for the many of today's larger landscape parks and gardens. The best known example is **Knole Park** where the present herd of deer is even attuned to the motor car.

Leeds Castle, Godinton, Cobham, Penshurst and nearby **Leigh** are other surviving deer parks with or without their animals, their planting altered as subsequent changing fashions dictated. Deer parks, whether owned by the church or the laity, have

always been symbols of wealth, and even those who did not hunt appreciated the visual attractiveness of a park landscape peopled with deer. This much can be seen from the innumerable mediaeval paintings, stained glass and tapestries, which also illustrate mediaeval man's liking for flowers. One has only to look at the stone carving at Canterbury Cathedral or the floral frescoes remaining at Rochester Cathedral to reinforce this point.

Despite later changes, the boundaries, banks and ditches can be traced at **Knole**, **Otford** and **Leigh**. The common oak, which formed the basis for the pre-Conquest Wealden forests remains as the predominant deer park tree. The most historic example, already marked on a map of 1769, and depicted in the process of measurement of the trunk circumference by **J.G.Wood** circa 1800, is the 450 -500 year old Fredville Oak, also called 'Majesty'. At the present time it is 11.9 m (39' 7") in girth, at 1. 5m height above the ground. At **Mersham-le-Hatch Park** there are many once-coppiced ancient hornbeams, the coppicing increasing both the longevity of the tree and its economic value.

Only the garden archaeologist can now trace the lay-outs of many mediaeval gardens of manors, castles or monasteries. Others are recorded in royal and monastic papers. However the existence of the latter sources confirms the significance of the church and the court in advancing skills in the cultivation of vegetables, herbs and flowers, whilst creating a garden pleasing to all the senses.

There is evidence at Canterbury Cathedral, of the

Fredville Oak at Fredville Park, East Kent.
Coloured late Georgian engraving by William
Green after drawing by J.G Wood. (by courtesy
of Kent Heritage Services).

once characteristic mediaeval enclosed garden or
'hortus inclusus'. It is in a manuscript drawing of
Canterbury Cathedral precinct, prepared circa
1160, for the primary purpose of displaying the
complexity of the piped water supply. In the south
east corner of the lesser cloister is what has been
identified as the *herbarium* enclosed within its wattle
trellis. Adjacent is an elaborately lobed fountain pool
under an arcaded roof structure. Illustrations of other
gardens tell of rectangular beds, often raised and small
enough to be cultivated from the surrounding paths.
Turf and turf seats were a luxury. Arbours or more
simple trellis provided shelter and support for climbing
plants or trained evergreens. At the **Archbishop's
Palace, Maidstone**, such a garden has recently been
recreated, following the example of the delightful
recreation within a confined courtyard at Winchester
Castle. At Knole the walled enclosure built by
Archbishop Bouchier at the end of the 15th
century still forms the boundary of the pleasure
ground and wilderness. Often the only indicator of a
mediaeval garden is this enclosing wall, the east wall
of the 1000 year old Westminster Abbey College
Garden being a splendid documented example.

Outside such walled enclosures orchards are
frequently depicted. The drawing of Canterbury
Cathedral Close has fruit trees and vines outlined
right at the edge of the boundary. In Tudor times
steps were being taken to include these attractive

features within the gardener's province. At **Hales
Place** the two corner gazebos of the Mount Walk
overlook the orchards as well as the garden and are
thus indicators of an outward expansion beyond the
hitherto confining walls. The gazebos also
symbolically represent the angle turrets of the outer
bailey of a castle, then a highly desirable symbol of
status.

By the time the moat, which so often formed the
immediate boundary of a mediaeval house had lost
its protective function, it had found a new ornamental
one, for water gardens were coming into vogue
following the fashion of the Italian renaissance garden.
The idea of the motte or raised mound was also taken
up in the Mount of the Tudor garden and was another
device for taking
in the landscape
beyond the
enclosed garden.
A painting of
**A y l e s f o r d
Friary** circa 1640
apparently shows
a tree-topped
mount near the
mansion, scaled
by steps.

Nowhere in
England can the
transition from
mediaeval to
tudor be followed
better than in

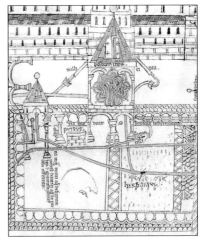

The herbarium and pool in Canterbury
Cathedral Cathedral precinct circa 1160.
(By courtesy of the Library, Trinity College,
Cambridge).

Kent, where, unusually, there are a number of gardens
that date from the late Tudor or Stuart period, which
are relatively little altered. By this period the renaissance
of the ideals of classical antiquity had enormously
extended the horizons of western European civilisation.
Moreover, these new Italian ideals were expressed in
painting, sculpture, architecture and gardens and in turn
these became models for the artists and 'cognoscenti'
across the rest of Europe. The resulting passion for things
Italian and the influence this had on garden design in
Kent form the subject of the next chapter.

CHAPTER 3

❦HINTS OF ITALY❦

B y the end of the 16th century Italian works of art were being studied at first hand by English travellers, for example the poet, Sir Philip Sydney of Penshurst, in the 1570s. Also prints of all kinds of works of art, including renaissance gardens, became readily available in England. Characteristically, Italian villa gardens were often dramatically divided into sculpturally ornamented terraces, sloping away or toward the house. If the latter was the case, the top terrace would become the Mount Walk for views beyond, as well as on to the main garden. Such gardens lent themselves as sites for theatre and pageantry.

The conversion of the older fashioned Mount to a 'Terras' at **Eastwell** near Ashford is refered to by **Lord Winchelsea** in 1702 as 'old Rome refined what 'ere was rude'. In 1663 **John Evelyn** made a similar reference concerning the garden of the **Commissioner's House, Chatham Dockyard**

The southern Tudor gazebo on the Mount Walk at Roydon Hall, with 17th century garden house attatched to the right.

'the pretty garden and banqueting house, potts, statues, cypresses, resembling some villa about Rome'. As so often is the case, the dockyard garden retains its terracing, but of the features actually described by Evelyn, only the banqueting house, in part, survives. Neither the English climate nor the English love of change aid the preservation of the characteristic urns and statues, so that the Italian inspiration is now less obvious.

At Canterbury Cathedral Library there is a remarkable coloured town map of Canterbury in 1642, which depicts many gardens in detail. The plan of Lord Wotton's famous garden at **St. Augustine's Canterbury**, which had been tended by **John Tradescant** senior from 1615, is outstanding, and of particular interest because it contained both new ideas from Italy and the currently fashionable knots and mounts.

Interpretation of the plan is made easier by a contemporary description (1635) of 'this famous place'. The walled enclosure of 20-30 acres was divided into five individual gardens, two of which were orchards while three had elaborate knots. One turns out to have been a lively water garden with an island, as then so much in fashion, and also created by Tradescant at Hatfield. It was full of statuary in the Italian manner, surrounded by a lime tree walk: *'in the middle of that sweet Garden, of fragrant, and delicious Flowers— is a neate and curiously contrived Fountain of pure cleere water, knee deep and four square, and in the midst, a little green Island and Charon in his Boat, upon the boat lies Snakes, Scorpions and strange fishes, which spout forth water about the Ferriman's eares and his Dog's, which is conveyed away by the turning of a Cocke. About it stands the Sentinells the watery Nimphs, on every Quarter'.* (See interpretation in chapter two).

Diagonally opposite lay an elaborate knot garden, while conveniently between the two was the 'Mount' with its characteristic spiral walk, from which to view the knots. Tradescant added a melon garden, then a novelty, and grew unusual plants, for example two varieties of Mandrake and a

Northbourne Court terraced gardens viewed from house site.

Turkish variety of the 'Indian Moly', *Allium magicum*. It is not known, but it seems likely that Tradescant designed this garden. There is no doubt he would have had the opportunity to familiarise himself with classical sculpture, through **Sir Dudley Digges**, the builder of the present Chilham Castle, with whom he travelled to Russia. The latter was a patron of the famous sculptor, **Nicholas Stone**. The classical correctness of Stone's style can still be judged by the Digges' monument at Chilham church and indeed Nicholas Stone provided garden statues and a fountain for **Oxnead Hall**, Norfolk in the 1620s. Collaboration between Digges and Tradescant seem likely during the creation of the dramatic terraced garden at **Chilham**.

At the former monastery of **St. Gregory's, Canterbury**, clearly shown on the map of 1642, there was also a well known garden 'with walks and mounts all walled about'. In the cathedral precinct a Mount had been fashioned on the site of the mediaeval campanile and two knot gardens are shown among

Bethersden marble inlay of flowers on a 17th century monument in Chilham church.

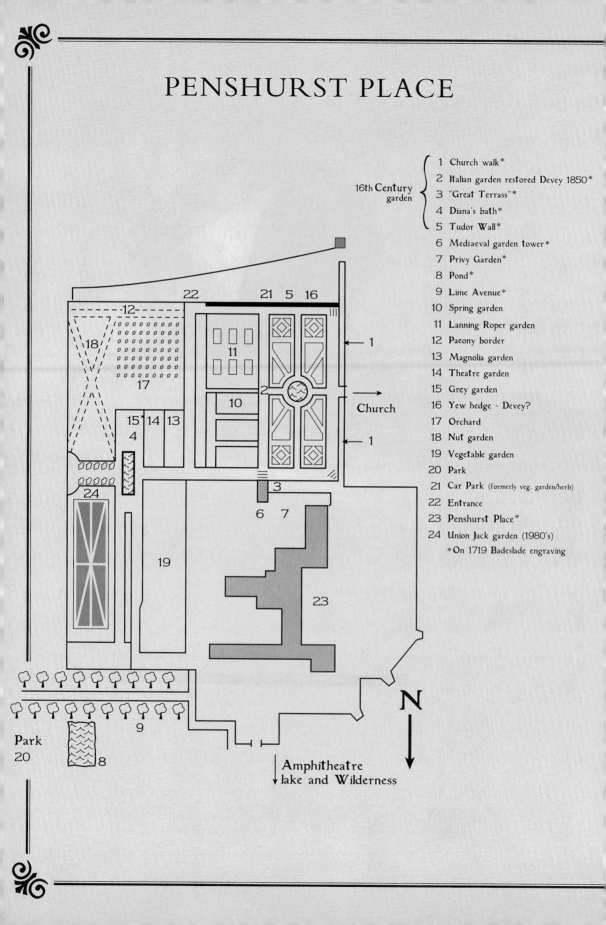

PENSHURST PLACE

16th Century garden
- 1 Church walk*
- 2 Italian garden restored Devey 1850*
- 3 "Great Terrass"*
- 4 Diana's bath*
- 5 Tudor Wall*

6 Mediaeval garden tower*
7 Privy Garden*
8 Pond*
9 Lime Avenue*
10 Spring garden
11 Lanning Roper garden
12 Paeony border
13 Magnolia garden
14 Theatre garden
15 Grey garden
16 Yew hedge - Devey?
17 Orchard
18 Nut garden
19 Vegetable garden
20 Park
21 Car Park (formerly veg. garden/herb)
22 Entrance
23 Penshurst Place*
24 Union Jack garden (1980's)
*On 1719 Badeslade engraving

22 21 5 16

12

18

17

11

10

15 14 13
4

24

2

1

Church

1

3

6 7

19

23

N

Park
20

9

8

Amphitheatre
lake and Wilderness

Survey of the park 1736 (John Bowra) copied Hugh Giles 1740

The Italian Garden

others in the town. A Rochester town map of 1633 depicts a walled garden to the north of **Restoration House**, Crow Lane, so the present Mount Walk in the back garden to the east may be a little later. No such delineations have been found for any rural area, but gardens actually surviving on the ground in Kent indicate further developments of the Italian style.

The most dramatically created example is at the site of the former Jacobean mansion, **Northbourne Court** near Deal, built for **Sir Edwin Sandys** by 1616. Here the garden is pure theatre. Within the hugely high enclosing wall of at least 15 feet, a Mount Walk runs along three of its sides, (the fourth was formed by the house), and above this at the west end, there are two further tiers of terraces to complete the theatrical effect. All of this excites the imagination, not least as to its underlying structure. The 'stage' now occupies the position of the former house. Apparently the acoustics are excellent for drama! No such ambitious earth moving or building of brick walls is to be found elsewhere, although sometimes the natural topography was used to similar effect, as with the terraces at **Squerryes** or **Ightham Mote**.

Both **Groombridge**, near Tunbridge Wells and **Hales Place**, near Tenterden have much lower Mount Walks, but at the latter garden the brick gazebos of late Tudor date now overlook an abundance of 20th century flowers set within the Tudor walls.

It is now a rare experience to be able to enjoy these once-common gazebos. A pattern for them is shown in the influential *A New Orchard and Garden* (1638) by **Gervase Markham**. They remained fashionable until the early 1700s, only to be revived in our own century for gardens such as **Hidcote**. Surely the earliest examples in Kent however are a remarkable mid Tudor pair of brick belvedere towers at **Roydon Hall**, near Maidstone, at either end of a Mount Walk, giving views down the terraces to the Hall and the panoramic landscape beyond. The southern tower has a 17th Century, two storey, brick garden house attached, with a heatable room on each storey, thus being suitable for entertaining. The gazebos at Hales Place are also two storey and multipurpose. The lower storey is appropriate for storing tools, the upper for enjoying the view and 'banqueting'. At that time it was the custom to partake of after dinner light refreshment in an outdoor apartment with a pleasant prospect.

The *'great terass'* of the famous

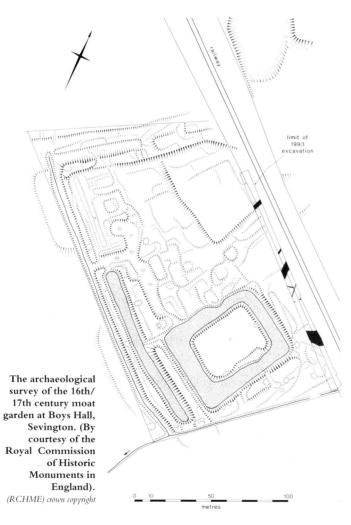

The archaeological survey of the 16th/17th century moat garden at Boys Hall, Sevington. (By courtesy of the Royal Commission of Historic Monuments in England).

(RCHME) crown copyright

walled garden at **Penshurst**, commenced in the 1570s, even before Sir Philip Sydney had returned from his Grand Tour, seems to have been without

One of the pair of two-storey Tudor Gazebos at Hales Place, overlooking both flower garden and the orchard without the walls.

such adornments. (See interpretation pages in this chapter). It gives an overview of the Italian garden, then called 'base court' which was being levelled in 1599, with *'walks thereunto pertayning'*. The excavations for the 'Gret ponde' had been used *'for creating the 'Terass'* at a cost of £24. 2s 11d.

Fruit trees were extensively planted along the walls, for example *'yellow peaches, apricocks, cherry and plum trees'* along the Church Walk. These formed part of the ornament. On the north side of the formal walled enclosure, an amphitheatre-like shape was hollowed out, the different levels being shown marked out by trees in 1719. By then, the large lake further north in the park was the focus of a small formal woodland garden or 'wilderness'. The lake is shown ornamented with a statue of Neptune on the 18th century maps, and there is a theory that this statue is now submerged beneath the water. A recent attempt has been made to dredge the lake in search of this watery deity, but so far he is proving to be elusive. Apart from the statue, it is notable that the above documented features are still recognisable. It seems very likely that the 'Gret ponde' is in fact 'Diana's Bath' shown on

the 1719 Badeslade print of the site, and located within the walled pleasure ground area. The expense involved in the original creation could suggest this.

In 1652, **Evelyn** commented : *' Penshurst, famous once for its garden and excellent fruit, stands also in a Park, is finely watered...'* How far the lost fame was due to the aftermath of the Civil War is a matter of debate, but certainly by then water features had become an essential element of English gardens. Presently many remains are being discovered and recorded. Once defensive moats found a new use, or were excavated where none existed formerly, sometimes foxing the present day archaeologist. **Groombridge** and **Ightham Mote** provide the finest surviving examples of such transformations in Kent, but at Ightham the water features in the form of canals and pools, were further extended to enliven the outer reaches of the garden. Recent archaeological field surveys have shown a similar situation at **Boys Hall**, Sevington. The archaeologist, **Paul Everson** describes its situation in the rectangular mediaeval moat, with canals and basons forming the focal point of the upper terraces of the late 16th or early 17th century garden beyond.

CHAPTER 4

❧ THE FORMAL FRENCH & DUTCH STYLES c.1660-1730 ❧

D uring the middle of the 17th century particularly grand scale interpretations of renaissance gardens were being conceived for the royal court of France, a fact well known to Charles II and his exiled court. The joyous creations of Louis XIV and his famous gardener, Le Nôtre, at Versailles, set the trend in Europe long before the garden's completion, in circa 1700. The fashion spread to Britain despite its autocratic overtones, which ran counter to the outcome of the Civil War. However few could aspire to the same levels of brilliance, particularly of sculpture and waterworks or indeed to the cost. Where Louis had marble or bronze, his English contemporaries contented themselves with stone or lead.

Formal garden at Deane Park, near Wingham with topiary and sculpture. (Badeslade 1719)

The many Badeslade prints of Kent country houses and grounds included in **John Harris** *History of Kent* (1719), reveal how far these new grand fashions had infiltrated by the second decade of the 18th century. Landscaping beyond the walls was expanded into the estate by the planting of great avenues stretching into the countryside, and vistas were opened up by the replacement of walls and fences with iron work grilles or clairvoyées. Splendid examples of the latter remain in the walled enclosure of **Knole**. **Badeslade's** prints show all manner of geometric layouts. Near the house, ideally viewed from the reception rooms on the first floor, there was often a division into individual gardens, with their parterres of broderie, probably brightly coloured using waste materials such as crushed coal, spar or brick, or grass plats ornamented by clipped evergreens and classical sculpture. There were also viewing terraces and walks, for the baroque garden was essentially to be discovered and enjoyed by perambulation. Water gardens, with or without fountains were known, and usually further away from the house, wildernesses of trees and shrubs, threaded through by cabinets, often ornamented with sculpture, and avenues which might give outward vistas onto the horizon. For **Goodnestone Park**, near Canterbury, **Harris** adds a note bringing to life the Franco-Italian character of the new design.

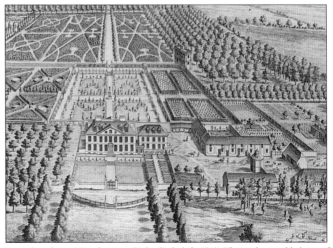

Formal gardens at Goodnestone Park. (Badeslade 1719) The twelve marble busts of the ceasars were as 'terms', buttressing two terraces of the west parterre

Terraces to the south overlook the former bowling green.

'Goosefoot' meeting point of avenues in the 'wilderness' at Chevening House.

'Brook Bridges hath Built here a very handsome house upon the ruins of the old one, and very much improved the Avenues and Gardens belonging to it, and along the sides of the Two Terras Walks, stands the Busts of the twelve Caesars in Marble, larger than life. They were brought from Rome and as I am informed cost there 600L'.

The only marble sculpture now remaining visible from the Emperor Garden, formely on the west side, is the handsome marble fountain bason and pedestal, the latter doing duty as a sundial on the east terrace.

For **Penshurst**, **Harris** describes the *'very large park which is adorned with long Rows of Oaks and Chestnut Trees'*. Such avenues could focus on the house from the entrance, line existing walks or be used in geometric patterns, over an extensive area of the estate, generating from 'stars' or 'goosefeet', still much in evidence at **Chevening**.

The intersections of tree avenues were often ornamented with a building or with sculpture. The confinement of limited boundaries and uneven topography that inhibited the full expression of the French style in Kent is somewhat disguised in the bird's eye views shown in Badeslade's prints. Indeed many find it hard to believe that the designs were actually carried out at all, in the complexity and grandeur shown, though evidence is building up to the contrary.

Le Nôtre himself sent a typical if rather plain design

for **Greenwich Park**, which was carried out. His avenues and the earthworks are still easily traceable on the ground as there is no overlay of a later date. Elsewhere the boundaries of some of the old estates are still traceable by the remains of ancient avenues, which form marked accents in the landscape as at **Oxonhoath**, near Hadlow. This is also the case at **Waldershare** in east Kent which retains, not only avenues on a grand scale, more akin to those in French gardens, but also a Wilderness, a feature still found at **Knole**, though here, unusually, not in the park but within the garden walls. Such wildernesses were also used for growing commercial timber, some even devoted to monoculture as were the 'chestnut' and 'ashen' wildernesses at

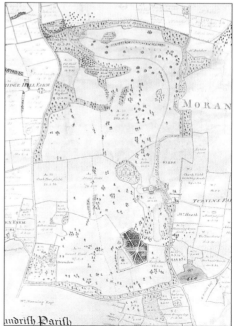

Survey of Chevening House Park by W. Woodward 1776

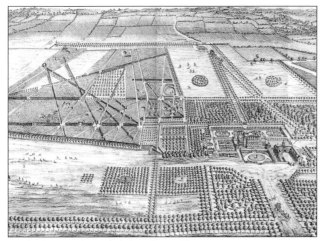

Waldershare Park. Badeslade print (1719)

Chiddingstone Castle.

At **Squerryes Court** near Westerham it is possible to discern how the terraced garden, created around 1680, was overlaid by the French and Dutch garden fashions immediately following. (See interpretation pages in this chapter). For even before the accession of William and Mary, in 1688, the Dutch taste in art and architecture had become fashionable in England. In gardens this manifested itself particularly in features such as topiary, delft ware containers for plants, and the use of canals to reflect garden houses as at the famous **Westbury Court**, Gloucestershire.

A coloured plan of 1686, displays the present, then brand new, classical mansion of Squerryes, overlooking terraces apparently dressed with vines, sloping down to two small pools. At the rear there is a long terrace on the southern slopes overlooking a canal, a grass plat, and parterre. Two important unsigned plans, one of them coloured, show that alterations were already planned circa 1706, and a Badeslade print of 1719 confirms that they were carried out. Avenues were extended into the park beyond the pleasure ground in the French manner, though of course on a modest scale compared to Versailles. Following the fashion in both Holland and France were the evergreens lining the pleasure ground walks, shaped into pyramids and umbrellas. Elaborate broderie parterres were situated at the side of the house awaiting their discovery by the visitor, while the new orangery (still amazingly in existence) was once reflected in its adjacent bason. It is intriguing to trace the bare bones of this garden today –in the terracing,

the remains of the avenues, and the double quincunx of limes neatly bordering the much enlarged canals. It is tempting to ascribe the plans to the circle of the royal gardeners, **George London** and **Henry Wise** of Brompton nurseries. Squerryes today is open to visitors, for details refer to gazeteer section.

The compartmentation of the original formal garden of the early 18th century with its enclosing hedges and terraces, has frequently determined the pattern of later gardens and can thus still be traced and restored if required. Good examples are at **West Farleigh, Ightham Court and Goodnestone Park**. At Goodnestone, for instance, they have recently replanted the west lime avenue, which ran between the two wildernesses. For here, as happened all over England in the 18th century, the formal

West View of Squerryes Court.

garden, so expensive to maintain, had been cleared to create a more natural landscape, modelled on the picturesque landscape paintings by artists such as **Claude Lorrain** or **Poussin**, which were often bought on the Grand Tour. The new style was held to form a particularly appropriate setting for the newly fashionable Palladian villa, while its freer more naturalistic spirit was seen as an expression of the current more liberal philosophical, political and literary ideals of the aristocracy and landed gentry. The informal Landscape Garden forms the subject of the next chapter.

SQUERRYES COURT

Westerham

N

Kitchen
Garden

The Tower

1. *House circa 1680
2. *Terrace circa 1680
3. *Upper terrace
4. *Canal, site of bridge
5. Canal, extension by 1735
6. *Quincunx of trees - mainly limes
7. Road realigned and sunk when
   canal extended
8. *Site of bowling green
   restored parterre
9. *Site of bason
10. Early 18th century sundial
11. Modern planting according to
    18th century plan
12. *Orangery - later laundry
13. Dovecot
14. 'Palladian' temple 1735. Eyecatcher.
    Viewpoint of house
15. Grove of Atlantic Blue
    Cedar. Mid 19th century, (by sluice)
16. Terrace
17. 20th century topiary garden
18. General James Wolfe cenotaph
    circa 1759

    * Features shown on
      Badeslade print 1719.

Design of circa 1706

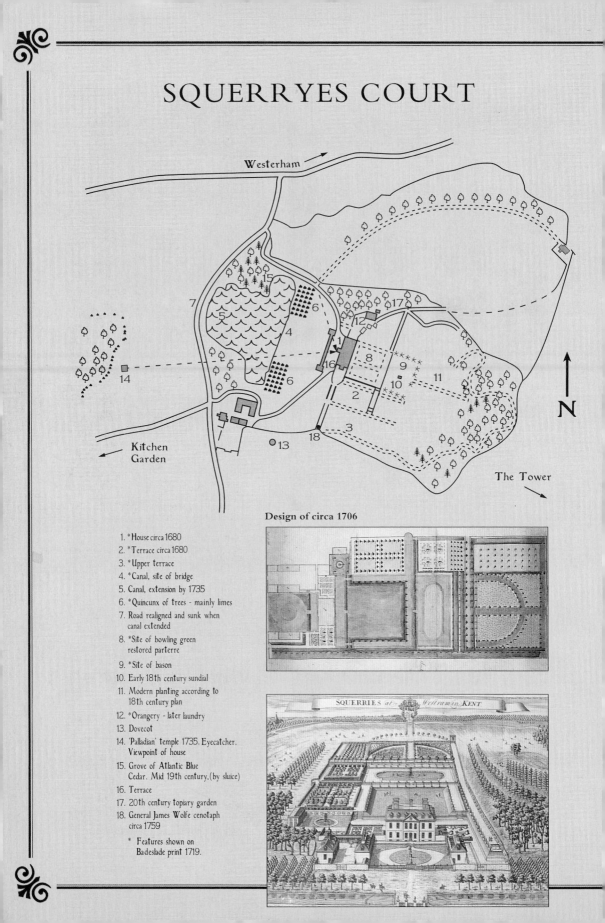

SQUERRIES at Westram in KENT

The east garden looking east

The family Warde by John Wootton 1735

CHAPTER 5

❦ THE LANDSCAPE GARDEN ❦
(c.1720-c. 1850)

One proof of the success of these 'classical' pastoral idylls that then became the rage, is the frequency of their survival to form a totally satisfying part of the characteristic English landscape, with their grazed lawns ornamented with specimen trees and clumps. The tree-framed mansion forms the focal point approached by an angled drive, or in later fashion, one that serpentines through woodland. The ha-ha, or fence sunk in a ditch, disguises the boundary between the lawn and the surrounding parkland or farmland, whilst acting as a barrier to unwanted animals. Often there is a lake, crossed by a bridge in the middle distance, with perhaps a temple silhouetted against trees on the hill beyond, as was so picturesquely added at Squerryes Court. The style depended on three of the country's best natural assets- forest trees, lush grass and ample water. So successful were the new creations that, by the end of the 18th century, scarcely any country in Europe was without its English Garden, as even the French had to admit. In Kent however, the transformation was not as dramatic as in many other counties, perhaps due to the population, of relatively high density from early times, and the smaller estates that resulted from this.

The pioneer works in the first half of the 18th century reveal a reluctance to give up formality and, as far as is known, none of the principal early practitioners of the new style worked in Kent. When **William Kent** (1685 -1748) was taking the first tentative steps towards naturalism in the grounds at Chiswick however, a second English copy of **Palladio's** Villa Rotunda at Vicenza was rising within its moat at **Mereworth Castle**, near Maidstone. The chain of canals north of the house survive while the formal canal on the south lawn, which was bordered by geometrically laid-out woodlands and a cherry orchard, extending into the park is long lost. A sequence of vistas and outdoor rooms was cut into these woodlands. A belvedere cum eye-catcher in the form of a dramatic ruined Roman triumphal arch, still forms an outstanding perimeter feature. It follows a pattern illustrated by **Batty Langley** in 1728.

Rather freer but still retaining formal elements are **Combe Bank**, near Sevenoaks and **Leeds Castle**, neither of which has been significantly altered. By 1748 the environs of Leeds Castle, dramatically set in its water-filled valley, had

Mereworth Castle (1720's and mid 19th century)

The eye-catcher cum belvedere on the southern boundary of the park at Mereworth Castle.

mile along a greensand ridge. A map of 1773 by **John Sparrow**, gives the positions of the vistas cut through the bordering groves of trees toward magnificent views of the lake, whose artificiality of shape is not yet fully concealed, and the wilderness (Park Wood) beyond. The promenade once terminated in a 'seat' (or temple) at the end of the artificial platform, giving fine landscape views. From here the route continues round the ridge with a complete change of mood, returning to the mansion through a dense grove of evergreen oaks and fir trees, and terminating in a gloomy grotto. The prospect opens up as the east lawn is glimpsed through rustic arches.

In Combe Bank there is a southern version of the great terraces and walks at **Duncombe Park** and **Rievaulx** or **Studley Royal** in Yorkshire, with their dramatic openings in woodland to give vistas of the castle, abbey or river. The site of Combe Bank had been bought by the Earl of Ilay, later the **3rd Duke**

been planted with mixed clumps, belts and specimen trees between the formal avenues. The canal and rivulet system wound its way through the park, but was semi-regular, and the cascades were, and still are, quite formal.

Combe Bank had a very important landscape setting, sadly affected by the 1987 storms. It was designed in full harmony with the new Palladian villa built from 1720 for **Colonel John Campbell**, later to become the 4th Duke of Argyll. He employed the Burlingtonian, **Roger Morris**, as architect.

The entrance front is set on a levelled lawn, framed by a raised walk sheltered by yews, once lined with great urns, of which four remain. There were trellis work 'seats', giving fine views of the parkland of East Lawn and beyond. One of these 'seats' survives, rather altered. In its original form it resembled those on William Kent's Bowling Green Lawn at Rousham.

The dramatically sited terrace on the adjacent side of the house at Combe, has more of a Vanbrughian character. It extends a quarter of a

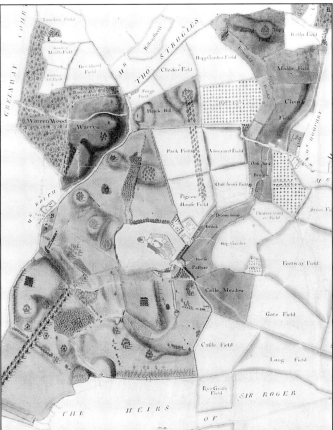

Plan of Leeds Castle Park by Thomas Hogben. (1748) (By courtesy of Kent Heritage Services).

COBHAM PARK

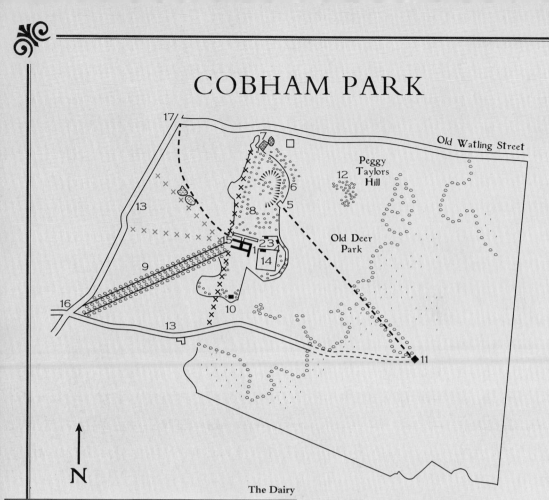

Old Watling Street

Peggy Taylors Hill — 12

Old Deer Park

N

The Dairy

The Aviary

1. House mainly 1584 - 1602
2. Antique Regular Terrace retained by Repton (in 1791)
3. Aviary pre-Repton*
4. Temple from Ingress Abbey* (* in Reptons irregular flower garden)
5. Site of Repton's seat Vista of Mausoleum
6. Remains of Repton's invisible fence running alongside old culvert or conduit
7. Old ponds including Fountain Pond and Pump House (1789) (originally mediaeval brick lined fishponds naturalised by Repton)
8. Old Garden (pre 1718)
9. Church Avenue retained by Repton
10. Dairy by J.Wyatt
11. Mausoleum by J.Wyatt c. 1789
12. Repton's grove (see Red Book)
13. Lane, boundary New Park of 1641
14. Walled kitchen garden (orchard in 1718)
15. Repton's flower garden
× Former avenues, removed Repton
16. Old Entrance
17. Present Entrance

The Mausoleum

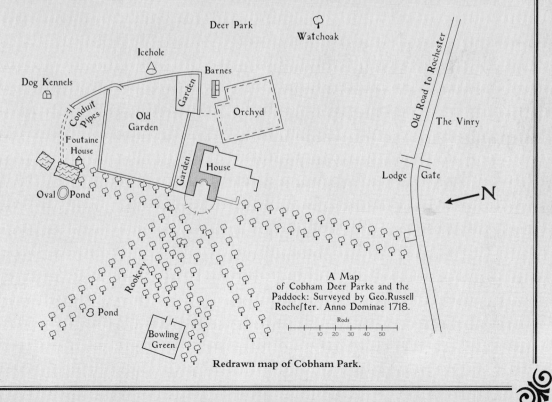

Deer Park

Watchoak

Icehole

Barnes

Dog Kennels

Conduit Pipes

Garden

Old Garden

Orchyd

Foutaine House

Garden

House

Oval Pond

Old Road to Rochester

The Vinry

Lodge Gate

N

Rookery

Pond

A Map
of Cobham Deer Parke and the
Paddock: Surveyed by Geo. Russell
Rocheſter. Anno Dominae 1718.

Rods

10 20 30 40 50

Bowling Green

Redrawn map of Cobham Park.

Early Georgian 'Terrass' at Combe Bank.

At **Lee Priory**, near Canterbury in circa 1780, Richmond created a lake which **Walpole** considered *'a humble stream improved'*, and added to the plantings of 'ancient elm', creating scenes that *'seem to form a site selected by Monks, much at their ease, with a view rather to cheerful retirement than to austere meditation'*. The parkland scenery remains, though **James Wyatt's** Gothick mansion has gone. Also in east Kent, **Samuel Driver** (d.1779) had at least two commissions to landscape in the 1770s, at **Goodnestone** and **Godinton** near Ashford. His watercolour presentation plan for the former (1773), shows the parkland ornamented with large roundels of trees framing vistas of the wooded hillside beyond, much as at present.

Robert Adam's Mersham-le-Hatch was designed in 1760 specifically so that the grandest rooms overlooked the expansive Stour valley. The scale and grandeur of the vistas of lawn, lakes with deer park beyond, and the rolling downs in the far distance, recall Brown's work at **Croome** in

of Argyll, who was then renowned for the laying out of grounds in a formal manner and for his cultivation of exotic trees and plants in his nursery. Could he have been the landscape designer for Combe Bank one wonders?

Capability Brown (1716-83), was to complete the break away from the formal style to create the rural idylls that so changed the face of the English landscape. His few commissions in Kent were at **North Cray, Leeds Abbey, Chilham (probably unexecuted)** and **Hill Park,** now **Valence,** near Brasted. Only the last, where he worked with his future son-in-law, **Henry Holland,** survives in part. Here Brown's engineering works of 1772 resulted in a picturesque series of lakes terminating in a twenty foot cascade near the entrance drive. A pump driven by a water mill was necessary to keep the system going. The notable lakeland landscape setting of **Danson Park,** near Bexley follows a drawing by one of Brown's fellow improvers **Mr Richmond,** circa 1763. The clumped drives are his individual trait, as has been pointed out by **David Jacques.**

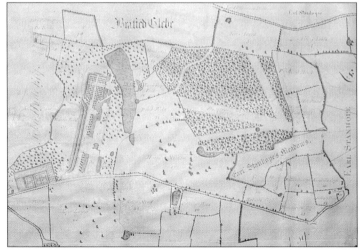

Survey of Combe Bank by John Sparrow (1773) by courtesy of the Headmaster, Combe Bank School.

Worcestershire. Did Adam –as at Kedleston–have a hand in the design?

The impact of the new movement on the landscape can also be enjoyed in the Nailbourne valley south-east of Canterbury, when driving along the A2! The almost adjacent estates of **Bifrons, Bourne, Charlton, Barham** and **Broome**, run together to their mutual advantage, giving the impression of a continuous parkland ornamented with specimen trees, characteristic clumps and shelterbelts.

After Brown's death his place was consciously filled by **Humphry Repton** (1752-1818), who developed Brown's 'natural' approach in a less stylised manner and brought flower beds and trellis work back to the environs of the house. He did more work in Kent than his predecessor and his famous **Red Books**, containing delightful watercolour sketches, displayed to potential clients the advantages of a new landscape. These books give us a greater insight into his working methods than is possible

with previous practitioners. Red Books have been located for the following properties, all in West Kent:

Bayham Abbey, Beckenham Parsonage, Blendon Hall, Bexley, Cobham, Crayford Workhouse, Holwood, Kippington, Montreal Langley near Beckenham, **Sundridge Park, Bromley** and at **Vinters** Park (Maidstone).

Repton's treatment of a Wealden river valley to form the focus of a landcape with ruins can be studied at **Bayham Abbey.** This transformation can be contrasted with his extensive alterations at **Cobham,** which is a large scale work amongst the renowned 'hanging woods and majestic trees' of a chalk hillside, but without a water -filled valley! Both works remain reasonably intact.

Repton publicised his Red Book plans for Bayham in a folio brought out for the purpose of self-advertisement. In which he reproduced the watercolours displaying his improvements. The 'before' picture, with the flap closed, shows the existing river valley landscape while the site for the

Bayham Abbey. Humphry Repton's coloured engraving with 'slide' closed, showing landscape before improvement.

Bayham Abbey. Humphry Repton's coloured engraving with 'slide' open, showing landscape after improvement. (by courtesy of the Lindley Library, Royal Horticultural Society)

proposed new house is amusingly marked by a chaise and twin posts on the partly wooded slopes beyond! On opening the flap or 'slide', a Gothick mansion, unbuilt until the 1860s, is revealed backed by characteristic 'fingers' of woodland, and overlooking the newly-created handsome expanse of water.

In contrast to Bayham, the **Cobham** seat was an ancient one, with a once famous garden, according to **Holinshed's** late 16th century report: *'one of the most notable gardens in the land, a rare garden - in which no varietie of strange flowers and trees do want.'* (see interpretation pages in this chapter). After Repton had worked for the particularly horticulturally-minded 4th **Earl of Darnley** for 16 years from 1790, he commented on his labours in the park, which though distinguished by its great trees and formal avenues, had been in a neglected state.

'Operations were begun by enveloping the whole of the by the rich foreground, over which they are seen from the terraces in the garden.'

One should add that Repton further ornamented the grounds with a judicious mixture of classical and gothick buildings.

His historic sense led him to retain the fine viewing 'Antique Terrace' to the north of Cobham Hall itself, with the added embellishment of a decorative bastion, and also the ancient avenue to the church. All other avenues were removed, replaced in part near the house by fine cedars and other specimen trees. He enhanced the pleasure ground walk, taking in the kitchen garden, whose walls were to be disguised by shrubberies as well as dark green paint! The partly new 'irregular modern flower garden' bordered the walled garden to the north. Here a fine focus is the aviary, a dressed flint building, present in 1758 when it served as a greenhouse. Repton also planned a

Danson Park, Bexley, across the lake. Landscape design by Mr Richmond circa 1763.

premises in plantations, shrubberies or gardens, its walls are enriched with roses and jasmines: its apartments perfumed with odours from flowers surrounding it on every side : and the animals which enliven the landscape are not admitted as an annoyance while the views of the park are improved

Winter Walk of evergreen trees and shrubs bordering the kitchen garden. Near the house, on the south and west fronts, Repton created borders for *'choice flowers and shrubs'*, the centre-pieces for the west front garden being two fine Coadestone urns and an

The 'Medici' Coadestone urn at Cobham Hall. (1801)

antique fountain. A contrasting rural vignette was formed by **James Wyatt's** carefully designed Gothick Dairy on the south lawn, alongside a rustic wooden 'Cow House' of Repton's own devising.

The slopes to the north of the 'Antique Terrace' were next beautified, and the rectangular Brewer's fish ponds enlarged. Nearby, Repton's picturesque Brewer's Lodge replaced a chinoiserie gate. Messrs Pilton's 'invisible' wire fences were erected on the boundary, to ward off the deer, and painted with an 'Invisible Green paint', giving minimum obstruction to views of Peggy Taylor's Hill to the east. This was marked out by new plantations. Repton rather irreverently suggested that James Wyatt's newly erected masterpiece, the classical mausoleum on William's Hill, be modified, to become a belvedere for viewing the *'busy shipping and inhabitancy'* at the junction of the Thames and Medway valleys–from which Cobham was a refuge!

Although now a girls' school, Cobham Hall and gardens are open to the public on selected dates during April, July and August. Further details are given in the gazeteer section.

The growing inhabitancy of rich industrialists in West Kent in particular, was to provide Repton and his successors with new clients. It also meant that the now much embellished landscape garden became the essential background for the typical suburban villa. Here the members of the new middle class could enjoy a 'retreat to nature' with all the convenience of being near a town and later a railway line. The resulting small parks, in principle, miniature versions of the landscape gardens, greatly enhanced suburban development. These gardens are a fast declining asset that can still be particularly well studied and enjoyed

Bastion by H. Repton.

at Tunbridge Wells, especially, in the earlier 19th century developments in **Calverley Park** and the more extensive gardens along Pembury Road, and also around Maidstone, Sevenoaks and the present day fringes of London.

CHAPTER 6

❧DIVERSITY IN THE 19th CENTURY❧

THE RETURN TO FORMALITY

T he expansion of villa development was very much the concern of J.C.Loudon, (1783-1843) whose horticultural publications were the mainspring behind that most influential organ among gardeners-the gardening magazine. His interpretation of the 'gardenesque' style resulted in a fashion for even greater enrichment of the lawned areas around the house. With the accelerating acquisition of new plant species, cheaper fuel and low cost but increasingly skilled labour, the most dazzling results could now be achieved, most often in a series of island beds, with vertical accents given by sculpture, water features or trellis. The diversity of garden styles and planting principles that he recommended included within an informally landscaped background, foreshadows the contrasting designs that were to be a characteristic of the 19th century. In Kent, Loudon designed, in 1835, the first public park in England-the Terrace Gardens of Gravesend, of which only rudimentary remains can now be traced. One of its attractions was an underground tunnel lit by fairy lights.

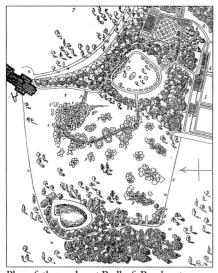

Plan of the garden at Redleaf, Penshurst.
From **J.C Loudons** *'Gardener's Magazine'* **(1839)**

Of this period, the once renowned **Redleaf**, near Penshurst is a remarkable survivor, albeit fragmented by 20th century housing developments, a fate also affecting many of the lesser known villa gardens of Kent. It was designed from the 1820's by the owner, William Wells, an ancestor of **H.G.Wells** and friend of the artist, **E.W.Cook** (later to work at **Biddulph Grange**). Here the island beds are edged in dramatic rock work, possibly intended to house the newly fashionable acid loving rhododendrons. Alpines too were grown. The paths are of bulky stone crazy paving and there is also a formal 'Dutch garden', a woodland garden and a lakeland area with rustic garden houses, a diversity characteristic of the period and all described and illustrated in **J.C Loudon's** *'Gardener's Magazine'* of 1839.

By 1840, when both the landscape gardens and the ideals that had promoted them were in decline, Loudon's complex informality also seemed incapable of further development. Thus a return to the formal garden of earlier eras found favour. The conjunction of an elaborate pleasure ground and a classical or newly fashionable chateau-like mansion seemed to demand a more geometric treatment. Hence the popularity, by the middle of the century of the formal 'Italianate style', with French overtones, as practised by **William Andrews Nesfield** (1793-1883) and **Sir Charles Barry** (1796-1860). Lawns adjacent to the house were stepped, where practicable, into a series of terraces

**Kitchen garden walk, attributed to Nesfield.
(circa 1847)**

ornamented with geometric parterre designs, bordered by stone or evergreen sculpture. These could then be readily viewed from the drawing room windows, as Nesfield had commented.

Among the numerous commissions won by Nesfield in Kent, was that at **Oxonhoath,** near Hadlow, which is undoubtedly the finest surviving example of his practice and the only unaltered Nesfield parterre garden in England. The original watercolour plan of the south parterre survives at the house, to display many of his customary devices. **Anthony Salvin**, while Frenchifying the mansion in the 1840s, had worked hand in glove with his brother-in-law,

Nesfield, providing viewing balconies from which to observe the 'broderie' designs on the two grass plats divided by a central gravel path. As usual, also in original French work, the coloured patterns were created using recycled material as well as fashionable plants. A last minute decision to edge the broderie in cast stone rather than box proved to be the key to its survival. In line with his standard practice, brick dust was used to outline the flower beds, and white pebbles surrounded the bordering rows of standard rhododendrons creating a truly dazzling effect. As in the early 18th century formal garden on the west lawn at Oxonhoath, sculptured evergreens punctuated the design, but the urns and mock fountain of cast stone are characteristic of the mid-19th century, and follow elaborate French patterns. Nesfield typically provided a bastion on a raised walk where the formal garden is separated from the landscape garden by a low stone wall and ditch to give fine views of the lake and the 'borrowed' Wealden landscape beyond. As the walk continues west the spectator is enticed toward the kitchen garden by the formally planted causeway that ends in a rococo revival gateway at its entrance, a charming Mediterranean touch. Oxonhoath is open occasionally under the NGS yellow book scheme and for some other worthy causes. See gazeteer for details.

Mid-Victorian Blashfield stone balustrade at Betteshanger Place, designed by George Devey.

OXONHOATH

1. House*
2. Nesfield, S. parterre (1847)
3. Site of Nesfield's rosarium
4. Nesfield, S.W garden
5. Cedar avenue
6. Nesfield, Kitchen garden walk
7. Kitchen garden
8. The Dell
9. Nesfield shrubbery (former terraces)*
10. Banqueting house* table top
11. Landscape Park
12. Viewing bastion
13. Bridge
(shown on Badeslade engraving 1719)*

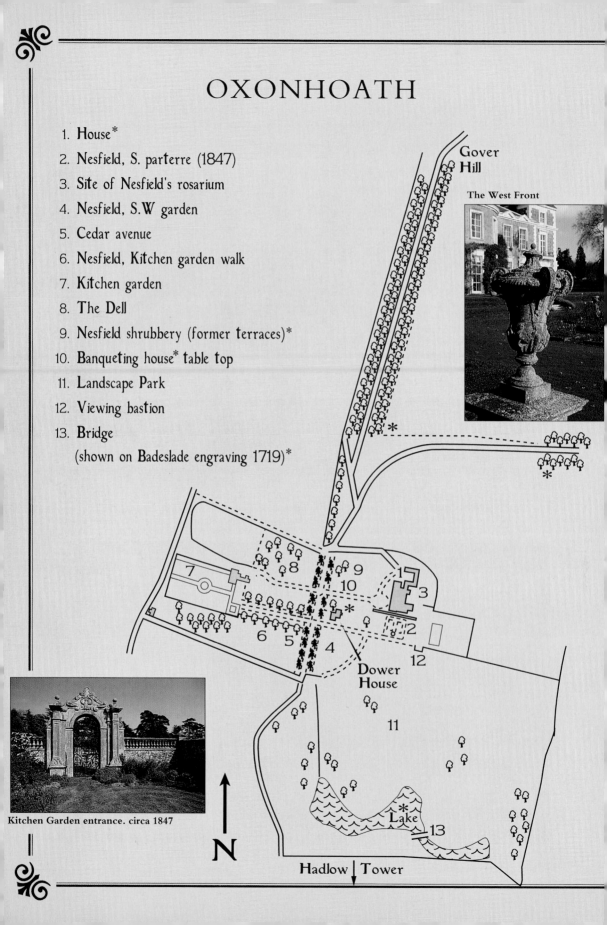

The West Front

Kitchen Garden entrance. circa 1847

Gover Hill

Dower House

Lake

Hadlow Tower

N

The South Front

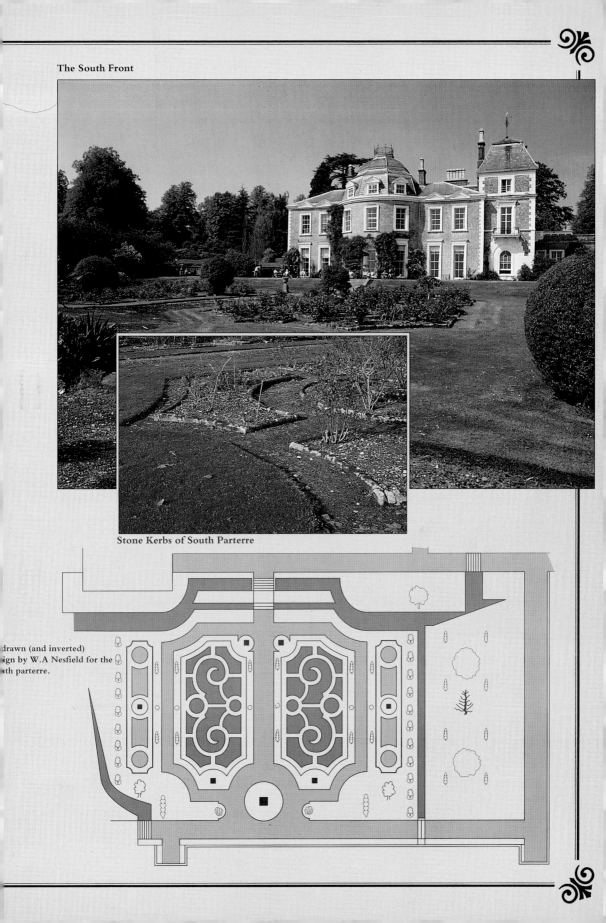

Stone Kerbs of South Parterre

drawn (and inverted)
ign by W.A Nesfield for the
th parterre.

Among many other estates for which Nesfield worked in Kent, his characteristic style can still be identified at **Linton Park, Bayham Abbey, Somerhill** and **South Park, Penshurst.**

Further notable examples of the formal style are provided by the gardens of the architect, **George Devey** (1820-1886). He was inspired by his early restoration scheme for the renaissance garden at Penshurst in 1850, which turns out to have been a pioneering venture. The same style of stonework as at Penshurst, can be seen in his terracings and steps at **Swaylands, Nonington** and **Hall Place,** Leigh. At **Betteshanger** he used the artificial **Blashfield** stone for some of his balustrading. His charming and idosyncratic cottage ornés are perhaps an undervalued embellishment in these landscape parks.

The popularity of **the woodland garden** waxed and waned. **Batty Langley** refers to them in the 1720s and his immediate successors certainly delighted in flowering trees and shrubs. The arboretum, as a specialist section of the garden, however, did not achieve particular popularity until the Regency period, when so called 'American gardens' were fashionable. It was not until the middle of the 19th century that the excitements of the new Himalayan rhododendrons, and the success of hybridisation with European species to give greater hardiness, became major factors in the development of woodland gardens. This idea was to be furthered by **William Robinson** from the 1870s, reacting against the current fashion of formality.

A rustic archway in the rock wall at Swaylands near Penshurst.

In Kent, **Scotney Castle** undoubtedly provides one of the earliest and at the same time historically most important survivals, for it represents a bridge between Regency and Victorian gardening ideals. **Salvin's** new mansion of 1835 for **Edward Hussey** is set in the High Weald on terraced ground sloping down to the romantic, moated castle. The latter was deliberately kept as an ornament. **Mavis Batey** has noted that the garden created round this now forsaken castle with its moat, and in the quarry made for building the new house, was **William Sawry Gilpin's** 'last glorious fling for the picturesque'. After his visit of 1834, the surrounding oak and beech woodland and the quarry were transformed by new plant introductions, notably the rhododendron tribe from the Far East, in the manner to become characteristic of Victorian woodland gardening. (These were further enriched with additional rhododendrons, azaleas, kalmias, maples and other choice specimens by **Christopher**

Woodland including a Wellingtonia, form the backdrop to the early 20th century terraces at Mount Ephraim.

Hussey in the middle of this century.) A typical mid 19th century 'marker tree' here is the Wellingtonia.

The woods of the greensand ridge as well as the Weald provide particularly good growing conditions for these gardens, at their most brilliant in spring and autumn. Their popularity continued to such an extent that they began to make an impact on some parts of the landscape of both Kent and Sussex. **Wakehurst Place** and **Leonardslee**, both in Sussex, are on the grandest scale. No less evocative is **Sandling Park** near Saltwood. In a few instances, such as the fine plantsman's gardens at **Doddington Park**, near

when grottoes were developing into the vehicle of display for newly discovered rock variations. By the end of the 18th century, mountains were no longer thought of as 'hideous', and nature was being eulogised by the Romantic poets such as **Wordsworth**. **William Robinson's** writing was equally influential later. The early but intriguing beginnings at **Redleaf** in the 1820s developed elsewhere into varyingly successful imitations of the alpine or even local peaks. **Paxton's** achievements at **Chatsworth** in the 1840s using monoliths are particularly striking. By the 1860s the rocks were

Scotney Old Castle, with its moat garden designed by W.S Gilpin (1834).

Faversham, or **Linton Park**, avenues of Wellingtonias or other evergreens planted in the last century add both colour and strong accent in winter.

The traveller's experiences in the European mountains with their glorious alpine flora proved to be no less stimulating to gardeners than the plant finds in the Himalayas, accelerating the growing interest in rock formations. This had been manifesting itself in various forms since at least the later 16th century,

being appropriately organised for the growing of alpines, perhaps most ambitiously from the 1880s at **Swaylands**, where Penshurst stone was used to provide two giant rock gardens, including caves, gorges and waterfalls and a quarter of a mile long rock walk !

From mid-century the ingenious **Mr Pulham** was able to find ample markets for his artificial rocks (waste materials covered in disguising cement, crevices and all.)

The easily created nooks and crannies were particularly beneficial for the then popular ferneries. **Pulhamite** can be discovered all over Kent, particularly in the **Tunbridge Wells** area and in the sea-side parks such as **Ramsgate** and **Pegwell Bay**. Rocky outcrops, artificial or natural, remained popular in all sizes of garden untill at least the second World War, while in recent years interest in grottoes has revived. This is currently discernible with the restoration of many historic examples as well as the creation of new ones, as at **Leeds Castle**, near Maidstone.

In considering the background to the ambitious scale and diversity of character found in Victorian and Edwardian horticulture one is led to ponder on the art and skills of the **professional gardeners** that scaled the summits in the ornamentation of both house and garden. A hundred years later it is only in the department of crop protection that standards have improved significantly.

Investigation of the walled-in kitchen gardens with their greenhouses and frames, reveals something of the gardener's essential and sophisticated back-up facilities, as well as indicating the range of cultivations. For example at **Quex Park**, near Birchington home of the Powell-Cottons, there survives virtually intact a walled greenhouse garden. The dates of erection are intriguingly documented on a painted board still in the potting shed. In 1902 when the 'recent improvements' had been nearly completed, the venture was described as exemplary in the **Gardener's Chronicle** (December 6) : *'the erection of new and comfortable bothies, fitted with all the sanitary improvements and modern appliances, from which many wealthy garden-owners might take pattern'*. Still intact in the potting shed is the Head Gardener's seed chest and desk, and there are substantial brick and tile fruit and vegetable stores. A boiler room, kitchen and a bothy also remain. One must remember that the unmarried gardeners lived in these bothies, not always in very satisfactory circumstances, for they

typically had to look after themselves. However, they were handy for stoking, ventilating and watering duties! Conveniently overlooking the bothies, the sheds and the brand new teak greenhouses and other glass, is the large Head Gardener's residence. Its scale and comfort symbolises the high status of its occupant, for in the past two hundred years the Head Gardener's practical, design and management skills had reached their zenith.

Each greenhouse and each heated and cold frame had a specialist function to help maintain the Head Gardener's 'all the year round service' in fruit, vegetables and flowers for the Great House. On the south facing wall, the other side of the sheds, the orchid houses (1901) merged into the vineries (1898), which also contained pot plants and some novelties from South Africa. Next came the peach and nectarine houses (1900), while the stove, older glasshouses and heated and cold frames filled much of the walled enclosure. A fernery (1898) was appropriately situated

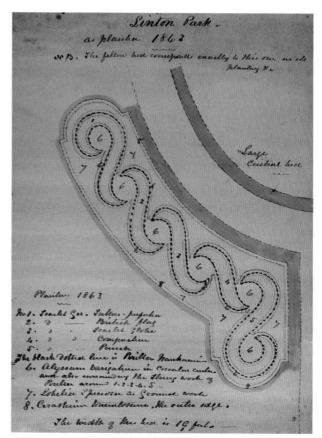

Fully annotated summer bedding plan for Linton Park by John Robson (1863). By courtesy of Kent Heritage Services.

The restored vinery at Quex.

Among other duties was the management of expenditure, including the sale of surplus produce, the purchase of seeds and plants, the creation of the floral arrangements in the house and the daily job list for his staff. Robson was indeed a highly skilled and at the same time, powerful figure. In 1873, the wages he paid varied from 8 shillings a week for the garden boy, to 14 shillings for the 'journey men', who, though under-gardeners, were usually able to take responsibility in carrying out most of the essential garden skills. The most senior men, who might be in charge of a particular department, such as the greenhouses, recieved the princely sum of 19 shillings a week.

With the advent of cheap imports of exotic flowers, fruit and vegetables from the 1870s onward and after two world wars which contributed to changing patterns in society, only a handful of gardens remain where the practices outlined above still apertain. Too often the responsibilities now devolve on one or two gardeners, although the fully intergrated tradition is still maintained at **Chatsworth**, as can be discovered during the Head Gardener's tours. It has been most carefully and evocatively recorded for the kitchen garden at **Cottesbrooke**, Northants in 1984, before that garden was temporarily abandoned. Plans currently exist for its reinstatement.

on the north wall, and the resourceful **Mr Cornford**, the Head Gardener at the turn of the century, had even dug caves in the chalk for efficient storage of roots and bulbs and the growth of mushrooms. He also grew 1,600 grand chrysanthemum plants of all the best varieties *'for exhibition as well as indoors.'* Cornford had a score of gardeners to assist him in maintaining his empire, which extended to a new three and-a-half acre walled fruit and vegetable garden, with another adjacent, as well as shrubberies inset into a small landscape park.

Further insight into the complexities of horticultural practice is given by the writings and diaries of the Head Gardener of **Linton Park**, from 1863-1874, **Mr John Robson**. At the height of the planting season he employed about the same number of gardeners as at Quex. The surviving diaries indicate the diversity of jobs, starting in January 1864, with an £6.2.10 expenditure on the ice-house filling *'all men that could be engaged thereon'*. Every detail of labour and cost is noted. An unusual job for the garden or 'crock boys' was to seek moss in the woods to wrap up the root balls of young geranium plants to minimise watering. However, the climax of work was in May, when all hands were in the flower garden then being planted up with elaborate new bedding. The bedding design was one of very many responsibilities of the Head Gardener.

CHAPTER 7

❖THE TWENTIETH CENTURY❖

JAPANESE GARDENS

To meet the growing desire to create 'genuine' far eastern gardens at the turn of the century, the specialist skills of the oriental gardener were employed. The developing interests in rock and water gardening had come together toward the end of the 19th century in a new guise-that of the Japanese garden. Interest in all matters Japanese had grown since the middle of the century. There was a great influx of Japanese plants from the 1860s, including bamboos, magnolias, camellias, maples, cryptomerias and Japanese yews, and early in the 20th century, the shapely kurume azaleas. In 1893, Joseph Condor (1852-1920) published 'Landscape gardening in Japan', which provided many analytical illustrations of authentic gardens. One of these designs has been almost literally copied within a typically Edwardian multifaceted garden, created by Hugh Micklem at Bitchett Wood, near Sevenoaks.

At Bitchett Wood the enclosed Japanese garden was designed by **Raymond Berrow** and laid out between 1919-21. Though now by Japanese standards somewhat overgrown, it remains intact and evocative. A large Japanese tea house in one corner overlooks a winding pool, crossed by three bridges and surrounded by a landscape of five grass-covered little hills. The paths are of stepping stones set in sand.

A japanese garden, model for the Bitchett Wood Garden, pl. XXV in J. Condor's *Landscape gardening in Japan* (1893).

The Japanese Garden of, Bitchett Wood, designed by Raymond Berrow (1919-21) and, modelled on a design in Condor's *'Landscape Gardening in Japan'* (1893).

Symbolism determines every ornament, including the obligatory stone lanterns, the well, the bridges, the 'view perfecting' yew tree, the umbrella arbour and exquisitely shaped boulders. The planting is almost entirely from the Japanese flora, notably cherries, magnolias, maples and azaleas–the latter until recently carefully pruned to form boulder like mounds. The water garden west of the lake diverges from Condor's model, but the Yatsu-hashi bridge of zig-zag planks, and some planting, such as hostas and bergenias, have of course the same origin.

A less formal arrangement of the standard ingredients at **Mount Ephraim**, near Faversham, still conveys the atmosphere of the gardens of the Far-East, but here, as in the other Kent examples so far recorded, it is relevant to quote **Lawrence Weaver's** comments on Japanese gardening in England; *'it only makes an English garden speak with a Japanese accent.'*

Japanese influence has pervaded gardening throughout this century, particularly as it fits in well with both the modern movement in architecture, and with display exhibitions. It was important in the early years of the **Arts and Crafts movement**, through which came encouragement and appreciation for local traditional crafts, vernacular building methods and traditional building materials. The consequence for planting concepts was that old-fashioned flowers or those of subdued colours found new favour. The movement is particularly associated with the Cotswolds where the wonderfully richly-coloured stone buildings and walls formed such a picturesque background for the new style. In Kent however the timber-framed yeoman's farms formed an equally painterly focal point and many were sold for conversion into gentlemen's residences. **Stoneacre, Otford, Pympne Manor** near Tenterden, **Marle Place, Great Comp** and **Crittenden** near Brenchley are typical. Of course **Sissinghurst** nearly falls into this category, but here mellow brick walls and Tudor cottages and barns form the foil for the planting, and the Tudor tower now functions as a belvedere.

The picturesquely timbered **Marle Place,** built in 1619 and restored from 1858 onward, follows the Edwardian fashion of diversity and contrast in specialised gardens both in form and function. For some hard landscaping the local ragstone was used, but a variety of hedging material forms the main boundaries. Characteristically at Marle, the basic outlines are formal, the individual gardens being of rectangular shape, with paths and vistas loosely arranged to link them together. For example the croquet lawn, the modern swimming pool garden and the Edwardian rose garden are inter-connected by a series of descending terraces. The elaborately

The Italian garden at Godinton Park, designed by Sir Reginald Blomfield (1916).

detailed Rose Garden in the style of the architect, **Inigo Triggs**, surrounds a sunken lily pool and forms the climax to the succeeding vistas. The two gardens modified for sports described above represent a popular twentieth century development. At Marle Place there is also a fine tennis court garden recently enlivened with a shrubby embankment. The popularity of tennis and swimming in particular gave the designer a new challenge in adaptation -not always met as successfully as at Marle, though occasionally in quite a spirited manner. For example at **Brattles Grange**, after the Second World War, a new 'oast house' was built to serve as a swimming pool changing room and the meandering pool was partly disguised by a handsome overhanging maple, convenience sacrificed for beauty surely.

Walls of clipped yew edge the Edwardian swimming pool and form the main outlines of the design at **Godinton** near Ashford. Here **Sir Reginald Blomfield** (1856-1942) created a series of new pleasure gardens round the brick Jacobean mansion at the beginning of the century. High yew hedges formed a counterpoint to the ancient walls to provide a firm boundary between the individual gardens or to channel vistas. The shaping of the yew echoes the gables of the house and the high hedging encloses a topiary garden, a pool garden, borders, a rose garden and Blomfield's latest addition in the 1920s, an Italian garden.

The best known practitioners in this period were however **Gertrude Jekyll** and **Sir Edwin Lutyens**, both of whom had a few commissions in Kent. Jekyll transformed a sunken tennis court at the **White House**, Wrotham (1919) into a shrub-bordered lawn, and some of her characteristic woodland planting could be seen bordering and overflowing a long series of serpentining steps at **Frant Court**, near Tunbridge Wells (1914). She also worked at **Stonepitts**.

Probably the least altered of Lutyen's work in Kent is the series of fine terraces at **Great Maytham Hall**, carried out for **H.J. Tennant** in 1909 -1910. (this garden was the inspiration for Frances Hodgson-Burnett's book 'The Secret Garden'). Though Italian in spirit, the originality of Lutyens design lies in his ingenious mixing of tile, ragstone and brick. At **Wittersham House**, which he modified, Lutyens designed a classical entrance forecourt, two formal rose gardens and a curving pergola. There is also an 'open air parlour' with decorative pilasters and niches in brick, set against an old wall.

Brickwork also dominates the grandly conceived walled enclosures and gateways of the generous terraces created in the first two decades of this century for the **Dawes family** at **Mount Ephraim**, near Faversham, to match their grandly extended house. The detailing is classical. Within and without the bold brick walls there is the characteristic Edwardian diversity of individual gardens, typically with fine views of the orchards, vineyards and parkland beyond. The Japanese garden is said to have been designed when one of the Dawes became bored with tennis, while **Waterer's Nursery** created the large adjacent

Vista through to early 20th century rose garden at Marle Place.

rock garden in the period beween the two World Wars.

Italian influence is never far away in England, and, as has been hinted above, was making a renewed impact in Edwardian times. This was perhaps in consequence of publications such as **Edith Wharton's** *Italian villas and their gardens* (1904). An unusual imitation of classical Antiquity appears in the

Hever Castle. The Pompeian Walk designed by Frank Pearson circa 1907

monumental Italian garden at **Hever Castle**, designed by **Frank L. Pearson** for **Lord Astor**. This garden is in marked contrast to his more traditionally designed herb, fountain, chess and maze gardens there. From 1903-1908 the architect worked in association with **Joseph Cheal** and Sons, the nurserymen. It was a mammoth project. The Italian garden is approached on either side of a semicircular bagnio, ornamented with a genuine, antique statue of Venus and classical columns. There is also an extensive 'Pompeian Wall' twelve feet high, designed in imitation of a Roman colonnaded forum.

The 'shops' built into the sandstone wall, are partially divided from one another by low walls and contain some genuine Roman artifacts from Lord Astor's large collection. They are cheerfully planted out with summer bedding, while the walls are festooned with climbers. The Italian theme, though closer to the renaissance pattern, is followed in the beautiful lakeside landscape at the termination of the

Pompeian Wall. The large expanse of still water forms the backdrop for a magnificent theatre and classical loggia flanked by columned screens. Fine lake views too are obtained from the long Pergola Walk, luxuriantly framed by wisteria.

On a much smaller scale **Thomas Mawson** provided a new setting for the splendid Carolean house, **Lees Court**, its formal beds complementing the strongly Italianate lines of the principal facade.

Another major Mawson work, a new garden for the mid-18th century Palladian villa at **Foot's Cray,** has almost entirely disappeared following the destruction of the house in the 1950s.

The Italian Renaissance is equally the source of inspiration for the steep hillside garden created for **Sir Philip Sassoon** by **Philip Tilden** circa 1921-23 at **Port Lympne**. The concept follows that of the great water gardens at Tivoli, only without the dramatic water works. **Rex Whistler's** delightful trompe l'oeil map shows how the hillside around the new house was sub-divided into a multiplicity of terraces, steps and stairs. Most monumental is the grand staircase approach to the house, with five pairs of landings, each one containing an individual garden. The serried walls of *Cupressus macrocarpa* dividing off the landings, now predominate. Below lie many more terraces, ornamented with fountain, flower or fruit gardens, while beyond is the wide open space of Romney Marsh and the sea.

Much of the detailing close to the house, which is now partly disguised by creepers, has a Lutyens feel. The colonnades either side of the Dutch Colonial style villa are designed to act as frames to the dramatic views, in the way that Lutyens used pergolas. The central wall pool and segmental flights of stairs recall Lutyen's **Hestercombe**. Tilden, like **Lutyens**, revelled in the grandly conceived swimming pool garden. Here it ornamented the wide terrrace below the house. However, Sassoon's enthusiasm for rich floral displays added a different dimension to the complex interlocking of vistas that is so important to Port Lympne.

Fountain in the courtyard at Port Lympne

CHAPTER 8

❦ THE PLANTSMAN'S GARDEN ❦

SISSINGHURST CASTLE

I talian influences were more subtly woven into the world famous garden created by Vita Sackville West and her husband Harold Nicholson between 1930 and circa 1950 at Sissinghurst Castle. Here yet more of the threads that run through Edwardian garden design can be identified.

Sissinghurst is essentially a dual creation, for on the one hand the husband wished to display a firm structure, while his wife overlaid it with her brilliant plantsmanship. As so often in Arts and Crafts designs, the individual gardens were either linked together by rectangular walls, in this case remaining from the Tudor great house, or by tall yew hedge dividers. The beds in the White Garden are differentiated by an abstract design of box hedging. The intriguing pattern formed by these various enclosures can be best enjoyed from the tower in winter and spring, when relatively devoid of plants. The diverging paths that form the all important visual and physical links between the 'outdoor rooms' then also become apparent.

However, in this now legendary garden which today is maintained by the **National Trust**, there is the great bonus that the original planting schemes are well known, and can still be appreciated never having been significantly altered. (See interpretation pages in this chapter). **Vita Sackville-West** followed in the tradition of **Gertrude Jekyll**, sharing her sensitivity toward colour combinations and her love of the older varieties of garden plants with their softer colours, particularly roses. She also followed her mentor in enjoying informality of planting, within the formal lines determined by the old castle ruins and her husband's landscaping.

She used her immense and ever developing knowledge of plant varieties to create the flower pictures of her imagination, crystallising it all in her writings. In consequence of this inspired effort, the idyll that was created became enormously influential, an important factor in the remarkably informed interest found among amateurs in England since the Second World War. Particularly well known at Sissinghurst, are the three individual colour gardens. The purple border in the Tower Courtyard and the orange/yellow South Cottage garden were created

before the War, while the particularly beautiful and influential White Garden in silver, grey and white tones, adjacent to Priest's Cottage, was planted 'under the first flakes of snow' of the winter of 1946. The central iron canopy festooned with the white rambling *Rosa longicuspis* was added in 1970.

The rose garden bears witness to Vita Sackville-West's pioneering work on the reintroduction of the Redoute roses, the hybrid perpetuals and the very early hybrid teas. Among these the lovely white Madame Alfred Carriere is dominant, as it clothes both Priests' Cottage and South Cottage. Beyond the formal gardens, but within the moat there is the informally planted orchard meadow, where naturalisation of bulbs and growth of wild flowers is encouraged, a feature so much promoted by **William Robinson.**

Few visitors (and there are many, especially during the busy summer season, when a timed ticket sysyem operates), go beyond these confines, thus missing the Poplar Walk leading toward the landscaped lake. (For details of opening times refer to the gazeteer section.)

A post-war garden created in the spirit of Sissinghurst Castle, showing the happiest selections

View of flower garden at Goodnestone Park looking northward.

of flower combinations, though within a simpler framework is to be found at **Goodnestone Park**. The background of the flower garden is formed by the mellow walls of the 18th century kitchen garden, with its Georgian rusticated archways bounded in one corner by a great Wealden house, while the long vista of the garden terminates in the grey stone church tower.

In this setting the spirit of the **Arts and Crafts movement** is followed entirely. Within the enclosure on chalky ground there are a succession of individual

The former hammer pond at Crittenden House, now a lushly planted water garden.

gardens, created by **Lady FitzWalter** and her Head Gardener, **John Wellard**, using a choice range of planting material. They include a silver and white garden, a yellow corner given contrast with tall blue *Salvia uliginosum*, an 'old rose' garden and a penstemon walk, where the planting is sensitively shaded between

the soft reds, pinks, purples and blues. Vertical accents in the various gardens are given by pillars of different clematis varieties, often misty blue in the Victorian manner. The latter are also abundant among the many exotic climbers on the walls. The kitchen garden department is edged with gay flowers, the centre walk picturesquely marked out with pairs of fastigiate yews.

The ideal of using a constantly widening range of plant material to make a painterly flower garden within an 'Old English' setting remains a dominant one in the second half of this century, to the virtual exclusion, in Kent at least, of the 'modern' style.

Where the topography and soil conditions allowed, plantsmanship could be dramatically, exercised in the **woodland garden**. For these brilliant, predominantly spring gardens, frequently only a department in 19th century designs, were often developed into a principal feature in the 20th century. **Hole Park**, near Rolvenden, a garden recreated from the 1920s onwards, is still in the earlier mode. The environs of the house were skillfully ornamented with a typically varied series of formal gardens, compartmented by old walls and yew hedges. The woodland garden, full of rhododendrons, azaleas and other exotics, was pushed forward into a woodland valley clothed with native beech and oak. It is heralded by an informal heather garden and a meadow full of naturalised spring bulbs.

In contrast, typifying the newer approach, **Captain Collingwood Ingram's** former house at **Benenden** peeps out amongst the trees of his woodland garden, also of the 1920s. The areas of planting radiate from the house in sinuous curves with islands inset in lawns. **Pympne Manor**, near Tenterden is intermediate in character. There are formal lawns to the south of the charming timber-framed house but the woodland shelters a lake immediately to the north, and it is here that the path to the woodland valley garden commences. Again the shelter of the native forest trees has been used for underplanting a collection of exotics that fill the naturally green canopy below the forest trees with blossom and colour, which is particularly intense in spring and autumn.

The cypress valley at Bedgebury Pinetum.

Whatever the variation, it can be said that the plans of woodland gardens are typically amorphous and are entirely dependent on the excitement of the planting to guide the stroller. The floral display often commences with *Corylopsis* and *Chimonanthis* species and other early spring delights, followed by cherries, both the large flowered Japanese wonders as well as the native *Prunus avium*. Then follow the far eastern magnolias, apart from the much earlier and very grand *Magnolia Campbelli*, with azaleas in the shrub layer. The pink, purple and yellow Himalayan candelabra primulas often outline the streams or ponds with the gigantic leaved *Gunnera manicata* as a foil. Rhododendron varieties contribute throughout early spring, but the majority flower in late spring. A succession of spring bulbs of every variety and hue make up the ground cover and lilies may follow in the summer. Often there is renewed life in the autumn with the brilliant colouring of deciduous trees such as Japanese *acers*, *Parottia*, *Cornus*, *Liquidamber* and the few deciduous conifers.

For those who seek winter interest, the **National Pinetum at Bedgebury**, established in the 1920s, provides an enormous range of handsomely grown conifers drawn from every part of the world.

In the present century gardeners have also been particularly drawn to introductions from South America, Australia and New Zealand. The vast increase in the number of varieties cultivated cannot be summarised here. Many can be enjoyed at **Mr Tompsett's** post-war garden of **Crittenden House**, near Brenchley, built up since 1955. Here the planting near the old farmhouse is arranged round the gnarled trees remaining from an existing orchard. Below lies the hammer pond, a relic of ancient iron workings, here turned into a colourful water garden and beyond is a woodland, partially cleared to introduce plants brought in by the owner from South America and the Far East, particularly the former. He also preserves some of Captain Collingwood Ingram's cherry collections. Particularly memorable is a planting of the fine white double 'Shimidsu' against a blue green South American mountain pine. Like Ingram too, Tompsett collected the mainly evergreen southern hemisphere beeches or Nothofagus species, which, when successful, make stately specimens. One of the finest in Kent is a *Nothofagus fusca* from New Zealand, in a small woodland garden created by Emily, Lady FitzWalter, in a freak acid patch, at **Goodnestone Park**, between the Wars. This garden continues to be developed in the present decade, notably with new plantings of *Eucryphia* species and small trees originating in Chile whose large white flowers emerge most welcomly in late summer.

SISSINGHURST CASTLE

■ Tudor walls or buildings
1. Purple border
2. White garden
3. Delos
4. Tower Lawn
5. Yew Walk
6. Orchard
7. Moat Walk
8. Herb garden
9. Nuttery
10. Lime walk
11. Rondel
12. Rose garden
13. Cottage garden
14. Exedra
15. Reserve garden (private)
16. Gazebo
17. Statue

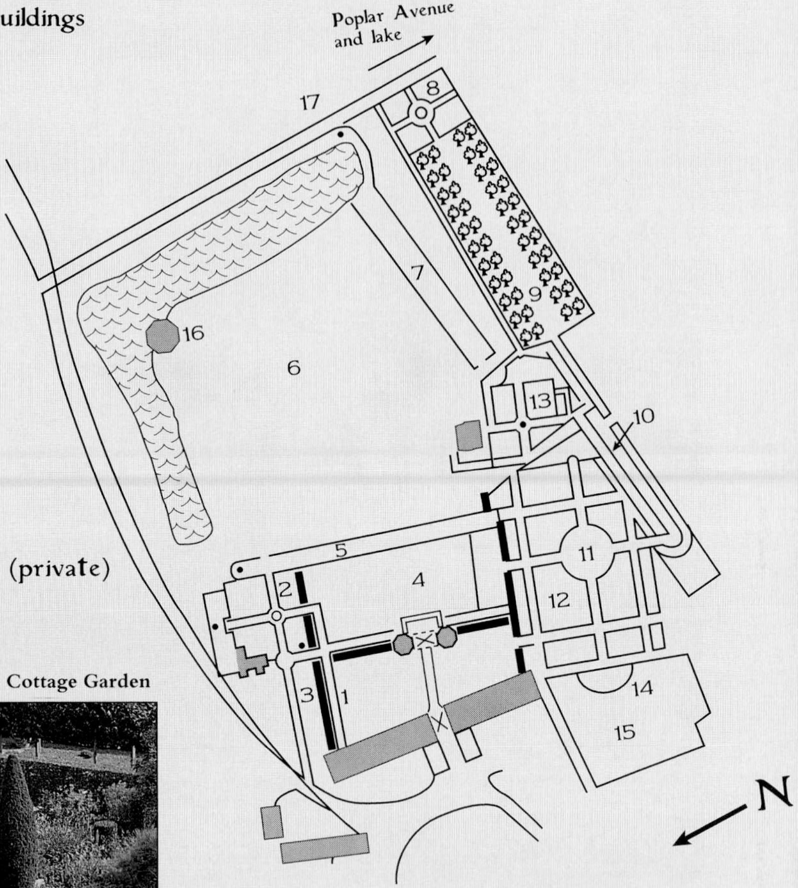

Poplar Avenue
and lake
17
8
7
9
16
6
13
10
5
11
4
2
12
3
1
14
15
N

The Cottage Garden

The Lime Walk

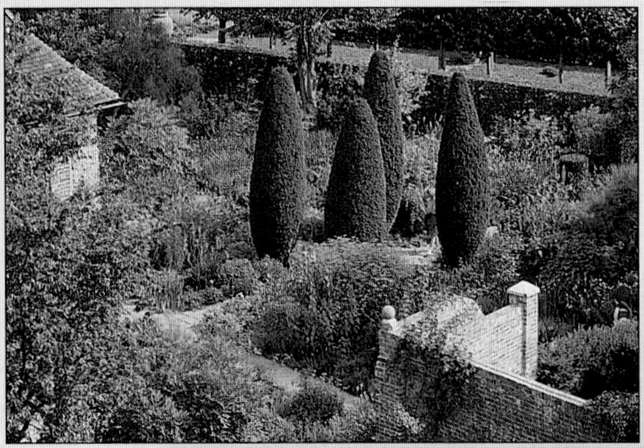

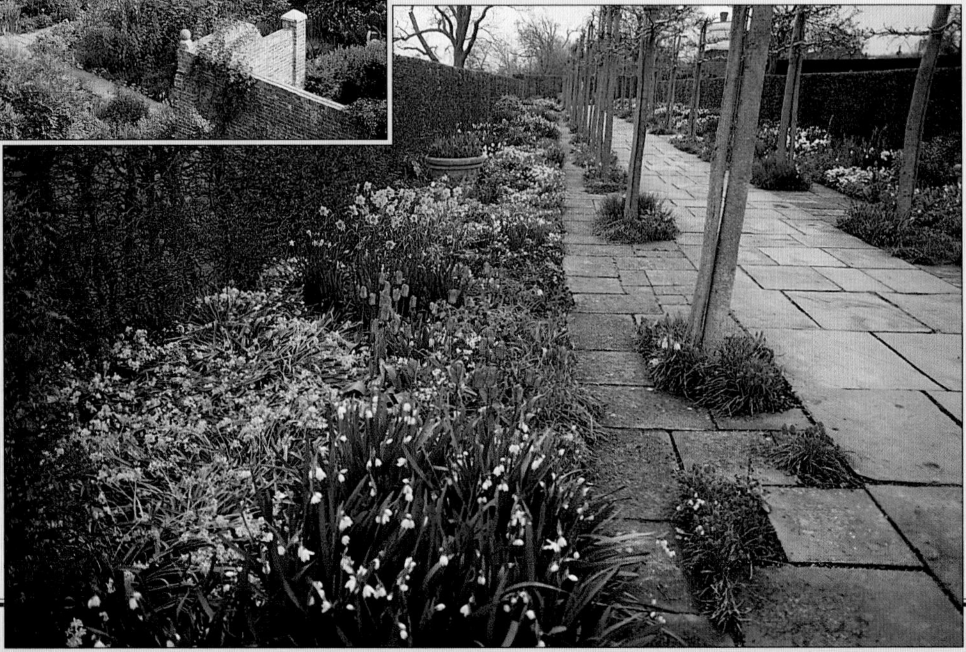

The White Garden in winter

The White Garden in Summer

CHAPTER 9

❧ CONSERVATION AND RESTORATION ❧

I n the last two decades of the 20th century there has been a resurgence of interest in the restoration or the recreation of historic gardens, sometimes facillitated by the emergence of County Gardens Trusts. In Kent, however, surely one of the earliest of all such exercises in England was carried out at Penshurst from 1850.

Penshurst had been rather neglected in the previous hundred years, fortunately for the preservation of the 16th century garden there. The young architect **George Devey** (1820-1886) was called upon to restore and extend the ancient mansion and to create an appropriate setting for it. He must have discovered that the underlying landscaping of the old garden survived. Such 'Italianate' terraced gardens were at that time again in high fashion. Adding his own version of appropriate stone work mouldings, he largely restored the interior of the walled garden shown in the Badeslade print of 1719, complete with the viewing terrace and parterre of the Italian Garden, the orchards and 'Diana's Bath'.

Devey was in advance of his time in appreciating the picturesque qualities of ancient buildings in their appropriate settings, but by 1884, when **C.E.Kempe**

seems to have commenced restoring **Groombridge**, near Tunbridge Wells, **William Morris's** principles had become well known and the **Society for the Protection of Ancient Buildings (S.P.A.B.)** founded. Thus it is not such a surprise to find Kempe restoring a barn into a billiard room rather than build an entirely new one, as had happened for example at **Oxonhoath** ten years earlier. Kempe was also commissioned to make a magnificent watercolour bird's eye-view of the garden lay-out as a whole, though how far its carefull detail represents fact and how much proposal is now difficult to ascertain. Comparing Kempe's plan with an 18th century estate map, it is clear that the mid 17th century terracing and basic compartmentation into individual gardens did survive. Thus, in all probability, Kempe only had to enhance and suggest new planting designs. One hundred years later his imprint is discernible.

However, even this restoration predates the early studies in garden history, which form an essential prelude to 20th century activity. One of the first to be published was by the architect, **Sir Reginald Blomfield**, whose book entitled *Formal gardens* came out in 1892. In this pioneering work

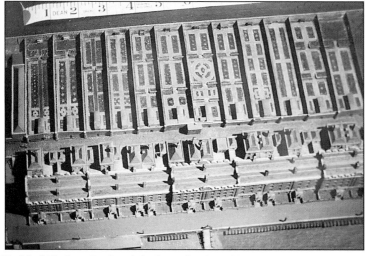

Model of Chatham Dockyard (in the National Maritime Muaeum) by William Phillips and John Monk (1773/4). Detail of Officer's Terrace gardens.

Blomfield included several Kent and Sussex examples in an analysis of the principal landmarks in the history of garden design. Indeed his appreciation of the importance of the Tudor gazebos and terraces at **Hales Place** near Tenterden has yet to be assimilated in the standard texts. As so often, commissions followed publications. At **Knowlton**, near Sandwich, Blomfield was asked by the **Speed** family to restore the Jacobean house and garden. He used the relevant Badeslade print of 1719 to recreate the individual walled gardens round the house, the foundations having survived as guidelines. The kitchen garden was retained in its original position adjacent to the house, and thus, though some of the functions of the newly recreated enclosures had changed, the garden had regained much of its old vitality.

A second landmark has been the publication of *Country Life* from 1897 to the present time. Its publishers also issued a series of beautifully illustrated volumes devoted to country houses and their gardens, whether old or new, and such illustrations have occasionally served as the basis for more recent restorations of missing features.

A century ago, few restoration projects were carried out with the strictest attention to historical accuracy. The great impetus for such an approach was not to take place until the foundation of the **Garden History Society** in 1965, which stimulated a new era of garden history research. Then followed the formation of individual county Garden Trusts. **The Kent Gardens Trust** was founded in 1987, just before the Great Storm of October. The devastation wrought by the latter unwittingly proved to be the real catalyst for garden restoration in the county. Wherever good parkland had been severely damaged, there was the possibility of grant aid. In the expert reports that followed the damage, the historic significance of some lesser known parks and gardens came to light and this has even led to restoration in some cases. An important example is **Combe Bank**, near Sevenoaks, where the great terrace and 'platform' for viewing the lake, are being replanted according to the map of 1773. Among well known gardens and parks that also suffered severely is **Cobham**, where there is now an ambitious programme for replacing

the wonderful range of specimen trees that once flourished there. The reports have revealed new information concerning the historic development of gardens such as **Chevening** and **Knole Park**. At Chevening, surviving 18th century plans used in conjunction with nurserymen's bills and the map of 1776, have been the mainspring for a long term plan of restoration of the wildernesses either side of the long canal.

View of the kitchen garden at Goodnestone Park looking southwards from church tower.

Such careful conservation is not possible without thorough preliminary historic surveys and the resulting accounts may indeed be the only record future generations will have of some important gardens. For example, the remarkable but declining ring of villa gardens around Tunbridge Wells deserve recording but most are unlikely to be restored.

An important new tool in achieving accurate records has been the development of both surface and underground garden archaeology, particularly to verify or extend information provided by documents.

Thus at **Knole** a canal shown near the Wilderness in the 1719 Badeslade engraving was recently excavated and has been recreated. At Chatham Historic Dockyard there are twelve Georgian town gardens of 1721-31, which were beautifully detailed on a model of 1773. Taken together these were a remarkable survival of the type, and archaeological

Chatham Dockyard. The Georgian fountain bason at No 12 Officers' Terrace.

rescue work revealed the paths, beds and steps and even a bason, exactly as shown on the model, and some of these features have now been restored or recreated at **no 1 The Officers' Terrace.**

The principle of accurate historic restoration is also not without problems. A decision has to be made as to whether to retain something of the palimpsest that most historic gardens have now become, or to restore to the most significant period in the garden's history. Often what is to be regarded as the most 'significant' period will be open to debate. This is a controversial issue, since **restoration**, rather than **repair** may involve the destruction of some of the site's historic and archaeological fabric. This issue becomes particularly controversial, when, for the sake of historical verity, the removal of fine specimens of forest trees, is carried out, as has happened at **Pains Hill**, Surrey. However even though there is much debate on this issue, the repair of existing features, of whatever period, within an historic garden, to ensure their survival, receives general support. This may be preferable to a potentially destructive wholesale 'restoration' to a single historic period.

Currently the movement to restore or recreate is slowly acquiring its own momentum. The first important recreation in Kent has been carried out with the construction of a 'mediaeval garden' at the Archbishop's Palace in Maidstone by the **Kent Gardens Trust**. It consists of a pattern of rectangular beds round a fountain, planted with appropriately chosen herbs and plants, and including, as at Winchester Castle, a tunnel arbour for shade and shelter.

Owners with original architect's designs or other surviving records, such as the Badeslade prints are much more aware of their value today. An example is the recent imaginative and effective recasting of the parterres at **Squerryes Court** for the Warde family, which none the less shows the creative hand of the restorer **Tom Wright**! Some motifs shown by Badeslade have been carefully reworked in box, but in the position of the former bowling green.

Currently a Victorian terrace is being restored at **Doddington Park**, near Faversham, following **Markham Nesfield's** original design. Terraces of two centuries earlier are hopefully to receive authentic treatment at the **Commissioner's Garden**, Chatham Historic Dockyard. The historic significance of the surviving, mainly Victorian greenhouse garden at **Quex Park** is fully appreciated by the owners, the **Powell Cottons** and their curators, Mr and Mrs Howlett. The latter are not only carrying out a restoration, assisted by a Kent Gardens Trust historic report and survey, but also ensuring that the garden functions in the manner intended. For instance the chrysanthemum standing ground used at the turn of the century by the Head Gardener, Mr Cornford to such good effect, is once again cheerfully ornamented in the autumn.

The achievements at Quex Park, as at some of the other sites being restored, would not be possible without a great deal of voluntary and unpaid overtime labour. For one of the problems of restoration is not only the capital outlay but also the upkeep. The designs being restored are practically always much more labour intensive than the existing ones. However, there is no doubt that restored gardens do add a new dimension to the understanding and

Chevening restored

enjoyment of garden history, as well as enhancing the buildings to which they were originally linked.

Anyone studying Kent's gardens cannot fail to notice how, often against all odds, maintenance is kept up. However, looking into the future, serious problems lie ahead, not least that the well trained and highly dedicated gardener is dying out as a breed. Even now the high standards still being achieved are so often due to the employment of superannuated gardeners or dedicated amateurs, often over retirement age. The demise of municipal park training schemes at a time when economic conditions preclude most private owners from taking on apprentices, will cause a serious decline in the number of skilled gardeners available, even if they can be afforded. Added to this there is the tendency in the more formal training establishments to substitute the managerial for the practical. On the other hand the **National Trust** training scheme is a relatively new and welcome development, but of course mainly for their own gardens. One should perhaps also consider the impact of the many gardening programmes on television, which do much to advise and inform. Again on the positive side, many a gifted amateur is taking over where the professionals have left off and in the present

time it is due to them as much as the professionals that gardening standards are being maintained and developed, particularly in the area of plantsmanship.

Of course, this new generation of gardeners can call on a much greater range of mechanical assistance, which is vital for the maintenance of the larger parks. The main problem of conservation in this area is that the majority of parkland specimen trees and clumps were planted in the 18th century and have now either disappeared leaving little or no trace, or are past their prime. Here the 1987 storm has proved a blessing in disguise and there has been much research to ensure that the historic patterns and species were retained in those parks worst effected. This leaves many, particularly in east Kent, in desperate need of replanting schemes.

A further difficulty is created by changes in ownership patterns. A rough survey has shown that, of the major country houses and gardens open to the public, only a handful in Kent are still owned, lived in and lovingly cared for by the families that originally created them. It clearly becomes much more difficult to resurrect a landscape where the mansion accomodation is shared between different owners, or has even been demolished altogether. In other cases, the picturesque idyll has been split up, and houses

Box hedge and espaliered fruit border at Mersham-le-Hatch Kitchen Garden.

built in various sections. The latter process is a frequent threat as country mansions come onto the market. On the positive side, at least there is a better chance that the individual sections will be kept up, even if the unity has gone.

Change from private to institutional use is often a saviour for the historic building, but may pose a threat to the grounds, as it is much harder to incorporate upkeep of the latter in any costing, when not strictly needed for the purposes of the institution.

A recent problem with institutional use concerns the changing role of local authorities. Now faced with drastic spending cuts, they can no longer afford to maintain historic properties, or keep them in uses for which they were intended. Such properties were often cheaply acquired after the war, and rescued from decay, but usually on shoe-string maintenance for the parkland.

Walled kitchen garden complexes offer a further particular challenge to conservationists. Their use to provide the complete range of fruit, vegetables and flowers for all the Great Household's needs once reflected social patterns, that is, a sharp concentration of wealth and comparatively cheap labour. However today these economics no longer hold true for local food production. This is particularly so in the face of the easy availability of cheap imported fresh and frozen fruit and vegetables. It is sometimes difficult to find new uses that do not destroy most of these sites' historic value. There is certainly an urgent need to record, preserve or restore representative historic samples, for example the remarkable hexagonal garden at **Chevening**, or the few still being carefully tended -such as **Mersham-le-Hatch, Chilham, Goodnestone** or **Quex**.

A growing public awareness and feeling of good will toward conserving historic parks and gardens now exists. Paradoxically, as the public's knowledge and interest have progressed, there have been cuts in available finance. In Kent however, there have been some promising developments. The most important survey is the **English Heritage Register of Parks and Gardens of special historic interest.** This volume is ever increasing in size to include the finest and most historic of the county's gardens. A 'listed' garden does not have the same statutory status as a 'listed' building, although recent government Planning advice (e.g **PPG 15**) makes it clear that the inclusion of a site on the register is a material consideration in planning matters. If the garden is listed 'II★' or 'I' it might become eligible for grant aid. **Kent County Council** has for many years accepted that a detailed appraisal of the county's gardens was vital before any general policy for their preservation could be established, and a number of important surveys have taken place, supported by the County Council, **Kent Gardens Trust** and the **N.C.C.P.G.** The results have been condensed into the *Kent Gardens Compendium*, a reference work available from many public libraries and currently (1995) being revised and a Public Parks report to be published.

The Kent Gardens Trust is anxious to increase its educational work in schools and has a formal programme which includes creating school gardens and providing teachers with information packs. The Archbishop's Palace at Maidstone's newly created 'mediaeval' garden is a living visual aid, while a practical aspect of the work is the adoption by several schools of the historic Captain's Garden at Chatham Historic Dockyard. The children will learn to maintain and enhance this, and other gardens, in line with the National Curriculum under the guidance of the Trust's Education Officer.

Practical conservation is much harder to achieve. Voluntary labour is vital, notably that organised by the **National Trust** and the **Conservation Corps**. A good start is being made in Kent with small scale projects, such as the repair of statuary or terraces within an individual garden. It is hoped that, with added public support, a more ambitious programme can be set up, thus ensuring that the achievements of the past will be there for future generations to enjoy.

Flower urn in tapestry at Sqyertyes Court

SELECT GAZETEER OF HISTORIC PARKS AND GARDENS IN KENT

KEY

- ✻ = Listed on English Heritage register
- NT = National Trust
- f = formal
- if = informal
- pg = pleasure ground
- P = park
- O = open regularly
- X = open occasionally
- E = hardly ever open or open by appointment

INCLUSION WITHIN THIS VOLUME OF ANY GARDEN DOES NOT CONFER ANY RIGHT OF PUBLIC ACCESS. DATES AND TIMES SHOULD ALWAYS BE CHECKED BEFORE A VISIT.

NB. **'Badeslade'** refers to the prints by Badeslade of Kentish seats and their gardens published in **John Harris'** *History of Kent* 1719.

BAYHAM ABBEY

nr Lamberhurst - (TQ 6436)

✻ f if pg P O

Fine landscape garden. **Humphry Repton** Red book 1800, for the **2nd Earl Camden**. Ruins of abbey focal point of lakeside landscape. Waving tree belt on northern slopes including many weeping beech.

Gothic mansion only built 1870-72. Victorian terracing (Nesfield?) overlooking lake, with pool and sculpture. Interesting walled kitchen garden

BEDGEBURY NATIONAL PINETUM

(TQ 7233)

✻ if P O

Early 19th century landscape garden converted into impressive arboretum 1925-6 by **Forestry Commission**. Some 19th century lakeside planting of conifers, also a pine avenue. Notable collection of Cupressus species. Experimental forest plots. Broadleaf trees in the valleys.

BELMONT

nr Throwley - (TQ9856)

✻ if pg P O

Samuel Wyatt villa and orangery of 1790 in handsome landscape park. Fine specimens on Lawn within ha-ha. Belvedere with Regency coloured glass. 19th century shrubbery and pinetum to west and north west of house. Late 19th century grotto in pinetum. Rose garden and rockery. 18th century walled kitchen garden.

The conservatory at Belmont House.

BETTESHANGER HOUSE
(Northbourne Park School) nr Deal (TR 3152)

f if pg P X

Mid-Victorian picturesque mansion for **Lord Northbourne** with formal gardens all designed by **George Devey**. Terracing and balustrades' round remnants of formal gardens. Grand staircase, **'Blashfield'** stonework, leading to **Salvin's** church and walled kitchen garden. Parkland. Characteristic Devey cottages on estate.

BENENDEN, (Hemstead Park)
nr Cranbrook (TQ 8033)

f if P pg E

Parts of Park Wood planted early 18th century. Formal terraces match Victorian rebuilding of Benenden House, with early 20th century Dutch Garden on east terrace. Pleasure ground to mid-Victorian designs by **William Broderick Thomas**. 19th century woodland garden with ornamental shrubs under canopy of deciduous trees and conifers. Lake, formerly fish pond, and ice-house. **George Devey** cottages.

BOUGHTON PLACE, Boughton Monchelsea (TQ 7749)

✻ if P O

Relic 17th century terracing to Tudor mansion overlooking grand views of the Weald and relic of deer park down slopes to the south. Lake and wet areas in place of 17th century canals. 19th century bowling green, lawns. Kitchen garden at least early 18th century (see Badeslade) in characteristic site adjacent to house. Thin rectangular shape. Walls of brick and stone. Paths bordered with box and espaliered fruit in 18th century manner.

CHARTWELL, nr Westerham (TQ 4551)

✻ f if pg P O NT

Terraced garden round remodelled farmhouse for **Sir Winston Churchill** by **Philip Tilden**. Marlborough Pavilion at N.E. corner of main terrace. Croquet lawn, herbaceous border. Extensive rockwork with descending pools. kitchen garden modified by 'Golden Rose garden' in 1958 and by **Lanning Roper's** shrubbery. East wall mainly brick by Sir Winston, with his studio adjacent.

CHEVENING, nr Sevenoaks (TQ 4857)

✻ f if pg P E

17th century house and pleasure ground overlook Darenth valley, backed by North Downs.
Essentials of southern pleasure ground early 18th century documented. Shows first developments toward informality :e.g. canal given irregular outline. Former bosquets 'round canal informalised late 18th century now being restored. Parkland running up slopes of North Downs later 18th century. Italianate parterrres, south and west of house laid out circa 1820, centred on Coadstone urn. Yew maze. Hexagonal kitchen garden circa 1775. Beehouse circa1850. later 19th century thatched apple store. Site of glasshouse garden.

CHILHAM CASTLE, Chilham (TQ0653)

✻ f if pg P O *(but for sale 25.8.94)*

12th century polygonal keep, 17th century hexagonal mansion for **Sir Dudley Digges**. Fine terracing overlooking deer park, possibly designed by **John Tradescant Sen**. circa 1620. The upper two terraces may have been subsequently modified and then reformed early this century. Striking topiary of various periods. Bowling Green lowest terrace. Quincunx wood and rockwork of doubtful date to N.E.. Mid 19th century lake marked by cedar grove. Woodland garden to south with early 18th century *claire voyée* giving onto deer park reformed 1733. Ancient avenues of lime and sweet chestnut. Old walled kitchen garden. Greenhouse wall flued.

CHIDDINGSTONE CASTLE, nr Sevenoaks (TQ4945)

✻ if P pg O

Former home of the **Streatfield** family.
Mansion extensively gothicised 1803-8, when grounds landscaped into present form to replace elaborate 17th century formal garden. 17th century wrought iron gate to Chiddingstone village. Lake crossed by stone bridge making a dam. Stone caves and rockwork cascade. Octagonal well house, also summer house and (shell of) orangery linked to house.

CHILSTON PARK nr Lenham (TQ 8950)

✻ f if P pg E

Landscape garden replacing formal garden (shown **Badeslade**). Visited 1660s by **Evelyn**. Lime avenue and several ponds from this time. Landscaped 18th century for **Thomas Best**. Late 19th century planting of ornamental trees and shrubs S.E. of house and Pine Avenue N.E

COBHAM HALL, Cobham (TQ 6868)

❂ **f** **ff** **Pg** **P** **O** *(school holidays)*

Mansion rebuilt 1584 -1602 for the 10th Lord Cobham. Garden renowned since 1577. Deer park since mediaeval times. Well documented garden development. Once one of largest parks in Kent – around 150 Hectares. cf. **Knole**. Present layout mainly **Humphry Repton** (Red Book) 1791-1816. Retained 'Antique terrace' (north) and Church Avenue. Designed formal gardens west, irregular flower garden east, plantations and specimens and clearings to highlight buildings old and new, as the Dairy **(James Wyatt)**, The Mausoleum (James Wyatt), the Aviary, the Pump House. Temple in irregular garden from **Ingress Abbey**. Formal garden south by **Goldring**, early 20th century. Walled kitchen garden and melon ground pre 1717, but built up with modern development. Although now a girls' school, open during selected days in April, July and August. Special tours can be arranged for pre-booked groups outside standard opening times, as can accommodation and food.

COMBE BANK, Sundridge (TQ 4855)

❂ **f** **ff** **Pg** **P** **X**

Palladian mansion for the **Duke of Argyll** with early partly irregular pleasure grounds circa 1730 onwards. Lawn east of house once bordered with rows of urns, a wooded bank either side terminating in two lattice work summer houses (one survives). West of house the 'Terrass' leads to the 'Platform'- a grove with views cut through to lake of 1745 and wilderness beyond. Two lower terrace walks, well planted, lead to 20th century rock garden and cascades, with 18th century grotto and tunnel beyond.

COMMISSIONER'S GARDEN (TQ7569)
(CHATHAM HISTORIC DOCKYARD)

❂ **f** **O**

Commissioner's House Garden. circa 1660. 17th century walls and part of terracing, 17th century banqueting house. 19th century ice house, (open to visitors) Royal Marines Garden and recreated 18th century fruit orchard. Restored KCC/KGT 1984-85.

CRITTENDEN HOUSE, Matfield (TQ 6543)

ff **Pg** **O**

Plantsman's garden created since 1955, 'round 17th century farmhouse and old orchard. 'Paisley pattern' beds near house, water garden in old hammer pond, rose garden, woodland garden. Many introductions from South America and Far East by owner and also from **Collingwood Ingram's** collection.

DODDINGTON PLACE nr Sittingbourne (TQ9457)

❂ **f** **ff** **Pg** **P** **O**

Formal and woodland gardens with 19th century park on greensand. Mid 19th century terracing around house by **Markham Nesfield** (plans survive). Sunken garden with rockwork by **John Dykes Coleridge** 1915 (plans survive). Woodland garden filled with rhododendrons, azaleas etc. replanting from 1965. Handsome Wellingtonia avenue. Walls of Kitchen garden.

EMMETTS GARDEN, Sundridge (TQ 4752)

❂ **ff** **O** **NT**

A greensand ridge woodland garden overlooking Weald. badly affected by storm. (cf. **Chartwell**.) Shrubbery north, rhododendrons, camellias, ferns. 19th century rock garden, alpines. Arboretum south including many specimens from **James Veitch and Sons** nurserymen, from sale of 1907.

FRANKS HALL nr Sevenoaks (TQ5567)

❂ **f** **E**

Mid-Victorian formal garden on lines of 17th century scheme. Four brick gateways from latter period. Also kitchen garden walls. Lawn with terraced walk. Paddock with specimens. 20th century knot garden. Italian garden and gazebo.

GODINTON PARK nr Ashford (TQ 9843)

❂ **f** **ff** **Pg** **P** **O**

18th century landscape park and 20th century formal garden within.
Samuel Driver (d.1779) landscaped arboretum and wild garden. **Sir Reginald Blomfield** designed formal gardens from 1902. Enclosed by great yew hedges and topiary. Statuary. Rose garden. Sorbus and cherry avenue. Sunken canal. Italian garden (1916) kitchen garden ornamented with treillage gates (Blomfield).

GODMERSHAM PARK nr Ashford (TR0651)

❂ **f** **ff** **Pg** **P** **E**

Deer park and 18th century landscape park enclosing pleasure ground. Mature lime and yew avenues. 18th century deer house and Doric Temple.
Ionic Temple 1935, with 'wilderness' beyond.
Norah Lindsay designed pleasure ground within walled kitchen garden in 1935. Italian garden with pool. Swimming pool and tennis court garden. Roses. Topiary garden. Old statuary.

GOODNESTONE PARK, nr Canterbury
(TR2554)

❋ f ff Pg P O

18th century landscape park enclosing skeleton of pleasure grounds circa 1704, when present house was built for **Brook Bridges**. Transformation of formal gardens by **Samuel Driver** (d.1779) Church Walk retained, made Serpentine Walk and roundels and belts. Amphitheatre style terracing west of west portico circa 1840. Woodland and rock garden 1920s-30s. Splendid flower garden within walled kitchen garden developed since 1955.

THE GRANGE, (Collingwood Grange) Benenden
(TQ 8032)

ff X

Woodland garden created from the 1920s by **Colonel Collingwood Ingram**, plant collector and breeder. Divided into series of glades. Japanese cherries mainly introduced by Ingram now in decline. Malus species and varieties, rhododendrons, azaleas, southern beech.

GREAT COMP, nr Borough Green (TQ 6356)

f ff O

Extensive plantsman's garden around 17th century manor house. Formal terrace Lawns, island beds. Woodland and heather garden, Ruin. Garden houses.

Great Comp.

GROOMBRIDGE PLACE, nr Tunbridge Wells
(TQ 5337)

❋ f Pg P O

Mid 17th century enclosed formal gardens to north of moated manor house rebuilt circa 1660 for **Phillip Packer**. Slope divided into three terraces; each in turn divided by central path: The lowest nearest the house; stream and lawns, the middle terrace; lawns herbaceous border enclosed by evergreen topiary, the upper terrace, once kitchen garden, lawns, shrubs, herbaceous border and statuary. Good gate piers and 'mount walk.' Entry from village marked by four Wellingtonias replacing Scots Pine. Parkland.

HEVER CASTLE, nr Edenbridge (TQ4745)

❋ f ff Pg O

Hever Castle restored for **William Waldorf Astor** in first two decades of 20th century. Gardens by **Frank Pearson**, laid out by **J.Cheal and Son**. around castle. Individual gardens viz: chess, herb, maze fountain and rose. Also rock and woodland gardens. Most striking is Italian Garden with Pompeian Wall like a colonnade with 'rooms' containing classical and renaissance stonework and sculpture ornamented with colourful plants. Pool. Loggia with outdoor theatre overlooking extensive lake. Regular public events, banquets, fireworks, concerts.

HALL PLACE, Leigh (TQ5446)

❋ f ff Pg P X

Victorian pleasure grounds and park, notable for fir tree collection, though much damage 1987. Formal gardens and lake with boathouse, probably by **George Devey** 1871-2, when he built the house for **Samuel Morley**. Walled formal gardens, topiary, fountain. Late 19th century rose garden and summerhouse. Mixed shrubs and herbaceous border, ornamental woodland. Mature oak avenue. Sunken area with rock garden, tennis court and pavilion.Very picturesque lodges by Devey in continental mode.

HOLE PARK, Rolvenden (TQ 8332)

f ff Pg P O

Early 20th century formal gardens, surrounded by parkland south east. Partly yew hedged, partly walled individual gardens. Rose garden, conservatory garden, herbaceous border, Eagle slayer statue (**John Bell** 1851 exhib) beautiful valley woodland garden, exotic planting (acid soil) among native oaks. Heather garden.

HUSH HEATH MANOR, near Staplehurst. (TQ7540)

❋ **f** **ff** **Pg** **E**

20th century formal gardens within woods. Circular herb garden, topiary.

Hever Castle - the theatre and lake.

KNOWLTON COURT, nr Betteshanger (TR2753)

f **ff** **Pg** **P** **E**

Pleasure grounds restored by **Sir Reginald Blomfield** 1904 using foundations of old garden walls depicted in Badeslade engraving for his boundaries. Sunken garden, terraces. Ornamental detail: Wrought iron gates, balustrades, sun dial. Avenue approach. Holm oaks abundant. 18th century walled kitchen garden cultivated.

LADHAM HOUSE, nr Goudhurst (TQ 7338)

f **ff** **Pg** **O**

Lawns with specimen trees. Fountain and bog gardens. Twin mixed borders, woodland garden with arboretum. Splendid views.

LEEDS CASTLE (TR 8353)

❋ **ff** **Pg** **P** **O**

Mid 18th century landscape park, much as recorded by **Thomas Hogben** (1748). Spectacular moated castle. Lakes, cascades. Flower garden by **Russell Page** within old kitchen garden walls. New maze, aviary and grotto. Public events, concerts, banquets etc.

LINTON PARK, Boughton Monchelsea (TQ7549)

❋ **f** **ff** **Pg** **P** **E**

Mansion of circa 1730 much altered in 19th century. Dramatically situated in 19th century landscape park on greensand ridge overlooking Weald to south. Very much developed in 19th century. Great beech and lime avenue on approach road north. Formal terracing south and south east of house attrib. **Loudon**, but may in part be mid-Victorian, due to **Nesfield**, with **John Robson**, the Head Gardener. Also from this period, Wellingtonia Avenue north west, Pinetum east, lime circle, rockwork and pool, grass amphitheatre, Gothic summerhouse, pair of gazebos, Magnolia Walk and a refit of the kitchen garden.

LONG BARN, Sevenoaks Weald (TQ5250)

❋ **f** **X**

Formal garden begun circa 1915 by **Harold Nicholson** and **Vita Sackville-West**, developed by **Lutyens** 1925, setting for mediaeval house and barn, in **Arts and Crafts** tradition.

Terracing, lawns and clipped drum Irish yews to South east. Delphic grove encloses swimming pool, reached by poplar avenue (cf **Sissinghurst** lake) Southern terraces Lutyens and Nicholson. Dutch garden of brick-edged beds.

MARLE PLACE, nr Brenchley (TQ 6839)

f **ff** **Pg** **O**

Characteristic Edwardian compartmented garden with emphasis on sport, restored 'round 17th century timber framed manor house. Plantsman's garden. Shrub borders. Edwardian gazebo, walled scented garden, rockery and pool garden, sunken Edwardian rose garden, swimming pool garden, tennis court and shrubbery, croquet garden. Lawns, specimens and yew hedge walk. Recent wild flower garden and herbaceous border.

MEREWORTH CASTLE, Mereworth. (TQ6653)

❋ **f** **ff** **Pg** **P** **X**

Originally moated, the 'Castle' designed by **Colen Campbell** for **John Fane** 1722-5. Now set in 19th and 20th century formal gardens surrounded by landscape park. Triumphal arch as eyecatcher now in woods. Traces of original formal gardens in canals and avenue to kitchen garden north of house. 'Rotunda' framed by ancient cedars. 19th century formal gardens in balustraded square south, formal beds. Evergreens, pool, good quality sculpture and two pavilions. 20th century formal gardens to east-lawn, bedding, rose garden, sunken garden.

MERSHAM - Le HATCH, near Ashford
(TQ 62 41)

ff P X

Seat of **Knatchbull** family, descendents the **Brabournes**. Deer park, ancient plantations, within 18th century landscape park, embellished when **Robert Adam** built new mansion 1760. Extensive views of lakes and Stour valley to north of mansion. Two lawns with specimens. Bordering woods contain ancient coppice hornbeams. Lawn south with Victorian pleasure ground. Wellingtonias, former rose garden etc. Walled kitchen garden, box hedge and espalier-edged beds.

MOUNT EPHRAIM, nr Faversham (TR0655)

✳ f ff Pg P O

Mainly 20th century pleasure ground, within 18th century and 19th century park, as setting for mansion transformed late 19th century by **Dawes** family.
Lawn and fountain (originally hydraulic ram). Large scale terracing with brick-walled enclosures. Early and extensive use of reinforced concrete 'stone'. Franco-Italian ironwork. Japanese garden, rock garden by **Waterers**. Lake and water garden (new). Fountain. Tennis pavillions (Restored 1995 K.C.C and Kent Gardens Trust). Regular public events, concerts, theatres etc. Fruit farm forms part of estate.

NORTHBOURNE COURT, near Deal
(TR 3352)

✳ f ff Pg P O

Most dramatic of renaissance gardens in Kent.
Early 17th century brick enclosure extending 200 metres S.W. of ruins of original mansion for **Sandys** family. Outstanding triple terrace at S.W end supporting Mount Walk. Theatre effect with lower terraces north and south. 20th century canal. Ancient yew. Walled kitchen and ornamental gardens. Tudor gateway. 1960s enclosed gardens, alpines. Park.

OFFICERS' TERRACE, (TQ 7569)
(CHATHAM HISTORIC DOCKYARD)

✳ f E

A set of 12 walled 'town gardens' and courtyards, contemporary with Officer's Terrace of circa 1721-31. 1774 model at Maritime Museum, Greenwich. Designs modelled still traceable;
Mostly terraced, approached by steps with cabin-like garden house over (nos 1 and 12), bason (12) stone steps, brick walls. paths. Evidence of many hothouses. Treillage in courtyards - some 18th century.

OLANTIGH TOWERS (TR 0548)

✳ f ff Pg P X

Mid 19th century pleasure ground within earlier park. Victorian formal gardens and large fountain, terminating in underground room. Statuary and urns. Woodland groves beyond. Early 20th century rockery and extensive water garden with island. American garden. Mount. Mid 18th century garden with circular wall.

OTFORD COURT
or **BEECHY LEES,** nr Otford

f ff Pg P E
Preparatory School

Late Victorian terracing around house with rhododendron woodland garden beyond. Use of Pulham stone in 'natural' rock garden. Model late 19th century walled kitchen garden with brick compost bin, complete range of bothies and head gardener's house, remains of greenhouse ranges and central ornamental well.

THE OWL HOUSE, Lamberhurst (TQ 6637)

f ff O

Woodland garden round timber-framed farm house. Formal gardens of terraces, flagged paths and borders near house. Pergola. Woodland garden. Rhododendrons and azaleas, rare shrubs under canopy of oak and beech. Water gardens developed from hammer ponds.

OXONHOATH, nr Hadlow. (TQ 6352)

✳ f ff Pg P O

17th and 19th century formal gardens within 18th century landscape park. Ancient mansion, much altered, on greensand ridge overlooking Weald. Of 17th century features, compartmentation, banqueting house table and avenues in park remain. Of 18th century, lake and bridge, specimen trees. 19th century Cedar Avenue. **W.A.Nesfield** formal gardens with urns to south and west and kitchen garden walk. 18th century kitchen garden walls. Dell garden. Open occasionally under NGS yellow book scheme. Sometimes by request for other causes. (01732) 810444.

PENSHURST PLACE, Penshurst (TQ5244)

✳ f Pg P O

Mediaeval deer park. Documented 16th century and 17th century for **Sidney** family -walled garden within. Many existing features traceable in **Badeslade**(1719) including Diana's Bath, lakes and avenues. Hollow of probable amphitheatre and bowling green (now cricket ground) survive in park to north. (Cricket ground first used in 1726). Restored **George Devey**, 1850. Post war gardens by **Lanning Roper** and **Lord de L'Isle and Dudley**. For visitor information telephone (0892) 870 307.

PORT LYMPNE, Shepway. (TR 1034)
🎌 **f** **ff** **O**

Early 20th century colonnaded mansion and Italianate gardens for **Sir Philip Sassoon**. Gardens by **Philip Tilden**. Grand entrance 'Trojan' staircase flanked by ramparts of Cypress, with stepped gardens adjacent. Courtyards. Circular yew hedge edged with niches for classical herms. Dramatic terracing south of house. Pools, fountains, chequerboard and marigold gardens, double herbaceous border Magnolia walk, fig and vine terraces. Zoo in woodland.

PYMPNE MANOR, nr Tenterden (TQ 8234)
f **ff** **X**

Formal garden and lake round former very picturesque timber-framed Wealden farmhouse. Woodland valley garden beyond. Heather gardens, lawns, and borders. Rhododendrons, azaleas and many specimen shrubs and trees in valley woodland.

QUEX PARK, nr Birchington (TR 3168)
🎌 **ff** **Pg** **P** **O**

Regency villa, Victorianised by the **Powell** family replacing Tudor mansion. Pleasure grounds within woods and parkland,
Lawns north of house with borders and specimen trees, notably a 'figwam' and a trained *Sophora japonica*, also rose border, within old garden. Sunken garden with pool on site of Tudor mansion. Important walled 'Glasshouse garden', mainly circa 1900 now being restored. 'Waterloo' bell tower in park. Collection of ancient cannon . Museum.

REDLEAF, Penshurst (TQ5245)
🎌 **f** **ff** **Pg** **E**

Innovative pleasure grounds of 1820s in Loudonesque tradition, laid out for **Mr Wells**, now fragmented by post war developments. Contemporary description and illustrations by **Loudon**.
South of house site, the rock garden, raised island beds, rock edged and 'crazy paved' path. Fernery further east. Dutch garden with brick edged beds. Rustic garden house. Redwoods. Walled kitchen garden, gardener's house.

RIVERHILL HOUSE, Sevenoaks (TQ5452)
🎌 **f** **ff** **Pg** **O**

Victorian pleasure grounds with contemporary plant introductions, including from **Robert Fortune** and **Joseph Hooker**. Greensand ridge views of the Weald. Terracing south, with wooden summer house. Rockery west. Walled, roughly terraced gardens to north. Rose Walk and ornamental shrubs. Woodland garden eastward.

ROYDON HALL, Near Mereworth (TQ 6651)
f **Pg** **E**

Remains of terraced 16th century garden for **Roydon** family. Pair of Tudor brick gazebos on top terrace (mount walk) and 'Henry VIII' clock tower. Front garden enclosed in zig-zag turreted Tudor wall.

SISSINGHURST, nr Cranbrook (TQ8038)
🎌 **f** **ff** **Pg** **P** **O** **NT**

Crowning achievement of **Harold Nicholson** and **Vita Sackville West** in **Arts and Crafts** mode plantsman's garden from 1932.
Semi-formal framework for individual gardens formed by 16th century castle towers, cottages, walls and moat. Special gardens: Red and purple, white and silver, orange and red cottage garden, roses, roundel, lime walk, herbs, exhedra moat and nut walks, Delos shade garden, poplar avenue and lake. Walled kitchen garden. **This garden is subject to severe overcrowding from visitors**, especially during June, July and August, when a timed entry ticket sysytem operates. Less busy times are weekday afternoons (4.30pm - 5.45pm) and Saturday mornings (10.00am - noon). There is some disabled access, including wheelchair loan. Coaches by appointment only. Tel: (01580) 712850.

THE SALUTATION, Sandwich (TR 3358)
🎌 **f** **E**

Early 20th century house and garden (circa 2 ¹/₂ hectare) by **Lutyens** for **Gaspard** and **Henry Farrer.**
Walls of flint, stone and brick. Lawns, terrace, herbaceous border. Drums of clipped holm oak. Water garden circa 1977.

SANDLING PARK, nr Saltwood. (TR 1436)
🎌 **ff** **Pg** **O**

Mid-19th century woodland garden, though house rebuilt after fire 1890s. Rose garden. Much additional planting since ownership of **Hardys**, 1897. Fine specimen trees, acid lovers. Rich spring under-plantings. 18th century walled kitchen garden.

SAINT JOHN'S JERUSALEM, nr Dartford (TQ5670)

🏵 f if O NT

Much altered mediaeval house on large moated site, occupied by historian **Edward Hasted**.
Within moat, walled flower garden, vegetable garden, nuttery, grass. Fine specimen trees. Woodland east of moat.

SCOTNEY CASTLE, Lamberhurst. (TQ 6835)

🏵 f if pg O NT

William Sawrey Gilpin's last commission designing terraces and woodland garden for **Edward Hussey's** new mansion by **Anthony Salvin** 1835, 300 metres up hill north east of moated castle. Native beech and oak interplanted with exotics, rhododendrons, azaleas, maple, kalmia etc. bog garden. Woodland dell in quarry. Ice well house, boat house, herb garden by **Lanning Roper**. Sculpture.

SOMERHILL, nr Tonbridge. (TQ 6045)

🏵 f if E

19th century formal gardens within fine 17th and 18th century park. Tree belts and specimens. Lake with islands. Formal gardens 50 m east and south of house. Grass plats, geometric division by paths. Yew enclosed bedding areas. 100 m. terrace and pergola. Natural shrubbery.

SQUERRYES COURT, Westerham (TQ4453)

🏵 f if pg P O

Outlines of formal schemes pre 1680 and circa 1700 for the new house built 1686 by **Sir Nicholas Crisp.**
Mansion on terrace west, facing mirror lake flanked by quincunx of trees. Remnants of lime avenue west beyond sunken road. Hilltop gazebo 1735. (Restored by **Kent Gardens Trust** and **Kent County Council** 1993) Main grounds east. 18th century orangery, modified. Parterres reconstituted on former bowling green, to be viewed from terraces south. Lawns, semicircular 'wilderness'. Topiary garden and rockery. 18th century kitchen garden with fruit stores in wall angles. Garden open sundays only during March; weds, weekends, Bank Holidays between April 1st - September 30th; and at anytime for pre-booked parties of over 20 throughout March - October. Tel: (01959) 562345/ 563118.

STONEWALL PARK, Chiddingstone. (TQ5042)

🏵 if P E

Valley gardens with streams on greensand. Canopy of oak and beech of Stonewall wood make shelter for ornamental planting of shrubs, waterfalls, pools, pond. Kitchen garden has flower borders and lawn.

SWAYLANDS, nr Penshurst. (TQ 4355)

🏵 f if pg P E

Victorian formal gardens and rambling mansion (with earlier core) by **George Devey**. Extensive rock garden. Devey created terraces south, circa 1870 (ornamental stonework cf Penshurst) overlooking parkland beyond ha-ha. Golden yew and oak specimens. Individual gardens -now mainly lawn- divided by rhododendron. Sunken rose garden. small arboretum north. Specimen redwood and Wellingtonia. Hidden giant rock garden north side of former upper and lower lakes, caverns, rock walks with niches-all Penshurst stone.

VALENCE, nr Westerham (TQ 4654)

if P E

House Victorian but earlier landscape park by **Capability Brown** for **Lord Hillsborough**, who paid £1200 between 1772 and 1775. Brown created series of lakes ponds and cascades running north south. Action by water mill, then hydraulic ram.

VINTERS, Maidstone (TQ 7756)

P O

Remains of 18th century landscape park, much of it now built on. **Repton** Redbook for **James Whatman** but only partly executed. Elaborate mid- 19th century terracing and rock garden (planting plan survives), and lime avenue/viewing terrace. House demolished. In care of Vinters Valley Park Trust and run as a local nature reserve. Some restoration proposed for ornamental gardens and vegetable gardens.

WALDERSHARE PARK (TR 2840)

🏵 f if P E *but public footpath*

Remains of early 18th century formal garden to house of 1712. Comparing with 1719 **Badeslade** engraving original features include oak and lime avenues (north east). Wilderness south west. Replanted but original criss cross paths. Iron screen. Belvedere (perhaps by **Lord Burlington.**) Parkland reconstituted after storm. 18th century kitchen garden.

WALMER CASTLE (TR 3750)

🏵 f if O

Late 18th century and 19th century formal gardens within ornamental woodland: Shelter belts, walled gardens and 'The Glen.'. Mid Victorian : gardens around central axis to castle. 'Broad Walk', terraces, with formal bedding. Yew alley remnants, Specimen trees. Remains of moat garden.

SELECT BIBLIOGRAPHY

Works frequently referred to in this book are:

Arthur Oswald *Country houses of Kent* (Country Life 1933)

J.T.White *The Parklands of Kent* (Shire Books 1975)

T.Wright *The gardens of Kent, East and West Sussex and Surrey* (Batsford 1978)

Allibone,J. *George Devey, architect (1820-1886)* (Lutterworth 1991)

Bisgrove,R *The gardens of Gertrude Jekyll* (Frances Lincoln 1992)

Bilikowski,C. *Hampshire's Countryside heritage-historic parks and gardens* (Hampshire County Council 1983)

Carter, G.Goode, P. Laurie, K. *Humphrey Repton landscape gardener (1752-1818)* Sainsbury Centre for Visual Arts. (exhibition catalogue 1982.)

Elliot, B. *Victorian Gardens* (Batsford 1986.)

English Heritage *Register of parks and gardens of special historic interest in England-part 24, Kent*

Harris, John *The history of Kent* (1719), including Badeslade's prints of Seats with their gardens.

Hartley, B and J *A gardener at Chatsworth* (1992.)

Harvey,J. *Mediaeval Gardens* (Batsford, 1981.)

Jacques, D. *Georgian gardens* (Batsford, 1983.)

Kent County Council. *Kent Gardens Compendium* (New edition due 1995.)

Leith-Ross, P. *The John Tradescants, Gardeners to the Rose and Lily Queen* (Peter Owen 1984.)

Morgan, J. and Richards, A *A paradise out of a common field* (Century1990.)

Repton, H. *Observations on the theory and practice of landscape gardening* (1803.)

Repton, H. *Fragments on the theory and practice of Landscape Gardening* (1816.)

Williamson,T and Taigel, *Gardens in Norfolk* (Centre of Anglian Studies 1990.)

Whittle, E *The gardens of Wales* (H.M.S.O 1993.)

Unpublished report :

Laurie,K. **Cobham Hall, Kent** Historical survey of the park. (1984)

ACKNOWLEDGEMENTS
by the author

I would like to acknowledge with grateful thanks the help I have had from many organisations and individuals among them the following :

Kent County Council Planning Department and Kent Gardens Trust, Kent County Council Heritage Services, Kent County Council Design Studio, Royal Commission for Historic Monuments in England, Royal Horticultural Society, Lindley Library, Trinity College Library, Cambridge, Chatham Dockyard Gardens Research Group, Adult Education Classes in Tunbridge Wells, Tenterden, Wingham, Sevenoaks and Gravesend. Among the many individuals to thank are : Jean Cobbold, Paul Everson, Marjorie Froud, Rachel Hall, Pamela Huby, David King, Pauline King, Tom La Dell, Jean Lear, Marian Liebeschuetz, Iris Smithwhite, Anetta Trothe, Gill Yerburgh, John Williams, my husband Ivan Hall who took many photographs, and the owners and curators of the historic gardens, without whose enthusiatic co-operation this book would have been impossible.

The inclusion of a site in this text does not imply unless clearly stated that it is open to the public. It is always advisable to check dates and times of opening before a visit. While every care has been taken in producing this book, liability is not accepted for any errors and omissions, howsoever caused.

INDEX

Allington Castle 11
amphitheatre 21
Arts and Crafts movement 4, 45, 50, 52
Astor, Lord 48
Avery Hill Park 7
Aylesford Friary 15

Badeslade, Thomas 22, 24, 25, 37, 56, 57, 58
Barham 33
Baroque garden 22
Barry, Sir Charles 36
Batey, Mavis 40
Bayham Abbey 9, 33, 40, 63
Belmont 63
belvedere 28
Beckenham Parsonage 33
Bedgebury Pinetum 53, 63
Benenden Grange 6, 11
Benenden (Hemstead Park) 64
Berrow, R 44, 45
Betteshanger House 37, 40, 64
Bifrons 33
Blashfield 37, 40
Blendon Hall, Bexley 33
Bitchett Wood 44, 45
Blomfield, Sir Reginald 47, 56
Boughton Place 8, 9, 64
Bourchier Abp 15
Bourne Park 33
Boys Hall 20, 21
Brattles Grange 47
broderie 22, 37
Broome Hill 7
Broome Park 33
Brown, Lancelot (Capability) 3, 32
Brook Bridges 24
Bunyard, George 10,11

cabinet 22
Cambell Col. J. 29
Canterbury 3, 9, 10, 12, 13, 14, 15, 16
Calverley Park 35
campanile mount 20
castle turret 15, 21
Charlton Park 33
Chartwell 8, 9, 11, 64
Chatham Historic Dockyard 16, 58, 61, 65, 68
Chatsworth 41, 43
Cheal, Joseph and Sons 48
Chevening 5, 10, 24, 57, 58, 61, 64
Chilham Castle 2, 9, 10, 13, 17, 32, 61, 64
Chilston Park 64
China 6
Chiswick House 28
chalk downs 7, 9, 10
Charles II 22
Chiddingstone Castle 25, 64
Churchill, Sir W. 11
clairvoyée 22
climate 5, 7
Cobham Court 5
Cobham Hall 4-6, 8-9, 14, 30, 31, 33-35, 65
Collingwood Grange 6
Combe Bank, 28, 29, 32, 57, 65
Condor, Joseph 44, 45

conservatory 63
Cooke E.W. 36
Cornford, Mr 43, 58
Cottesbrooke Hall 43
'Country Life' 57
Crayford Workhouse 33
Crittenden House 8, 9, 45, 52, 53, 65
Croome 32

David, Abbé Armand 6
Danson Park 32, 34
Darnley E. of 34
Dawes family 47
deer park 3, 14
Devey, George 18, 37, 40, 56
Digges, Sir D 10, 17
Doddington Park 9 41, 58, 65
Driver, Samuel 32
Drummond, George 8
Dunorlan 8
Dutch 22, 36
Dillenius J.J. 10

Eastwell 16
Emmetts 8, 65
Evelyn, John 10, 16, 21

FitzWalter family 52, 53
Fishbourne Palace 3
Foot's Cray 48
Fortune, Robert 6
France 3, 5, 22
Franks Hall 65
Fredville Oak 14, 15
Frant Court 47
fruit growing 3, 5, 11

garden centre 7
Garden History Society (Foreword and) 57
gazebo 3, 15, 20, 57
geology 5, 7, 9
Gerard, Thomas 10
Gilpin, W.S 40, 41
Godinton Park 14, 32, 46, 47, 65
Goodnestone Park 8, 22, 25, 32, 51, 52, 53, 66
Godmersham Park 65
'goosefeet' 24
grass plat 22, 25, 37
Gravesend 36
greensand 8, 9, 41
Great Comp 45, 66
Great Maytham Hall 47
Groombridge Place 3, 8, 9, 20, 21, 56, 66
Greenwich Park 24

ha-ha 28
Hales Place, Tenterden 3, 15, 21
Hall Barn 11
Hardy Plant Society 7
Harris, John 22, 24
Hall Place, Leigh 40, 66
hammer pond 8, 53
Henry, Augustine 6
Hestercombe 48
Hever Castle 4, 48, 66, 67
Hidcote 20
Himalayas 6, 40, 53
Hill Park 32

Hole Park 8, 52, 66
Hole, Dean 11
Holinshed, S.R. 34
Holland, Henry 32
Holwood 33
Hush Heath Manor 67
Hussey, Christopher 41
Hussey, Edward 40

Ightham Court 25
Ightham Mote 3, 9, 21
Ingram, Captain C. 6, 11, 52, 53
Italianate style 15, 16, 36, 48, 56
Italy 3, 4, 5 16, 24

Japan 6, 11, 44
Japanese garden 44, 45, 54, 47
Jekyll, G 4, 47, 50
Johnson, Thomas 10

Kempe, C.E. 56
Kent County Council 42, 61, 68, 70
Kent Gardens Trust 4, 56, 57, 58, 61, 68, 70
Kent, William 28, 29
Kennedy, Lewis 5
Kew gardens 4
Kippington 33
kitchen garden 7, 34, 37, 38
Knatchbull, Sir W 10
Knole 9, 14, 15, 24, 57, 58
knot 3, 12, 16, 17, 18
Knowlton Court 5, 57, 67

Ladham House 67
Lambarde 5, 14
Lambeth 5, 10
Langley, Batty 40
landscape garden 3, 6, 25, 28, 37
Lee Priory 32
Leeds Abbey 32
Leeds Castle 9, 10, 14, 28, 42, 67
Lees Court 48
Leigh Place 6, 14
Leonardslee 8, 41
Linton Park 7, 8, 9, 10, 40 41, 42, 43, 67
London, Regent's Park 4
London, George 25
Long Barn 67
Lorraine, Claude 25
Loudon, J.C. 36
Louis XIV 22
Lutyens Sir Edwin 47, 48

Maidstone 3, 15, 20, 35, 58, 61
Markham, G 20
Marle Place 8, 9, 45
Mawson, Thomas 48
Medway valley 3, 5
melon garden 17
Meopham 10
Mereworth Castle 28, 29, 67
Mersham-le-Hatch 9, 10, 14, 32, 60, 61, 68
Micklem, H 44
M25 motorway 8
Mount Walk 17, 20
mount 3, 12, 15, 16, 17
Morocco 6
Morris, Roger 29

Morris, William 56
Mount Ephraim 45, 47, 68

Nailbourne valley 10, 33
N. C.C.P.G 7, 61
National Rose Society 11
Neptune 21
Nesfield, M 58
Nesfield, W.A 4, 36, 38, 39, 40
New Zealand 6, 53
Nicholson, H 11, 50
Nonington 40
Northbourne Court 3, 9, 20, 68
North Cray 32
Nôtre, Le 22, 24
nurseries 5
Nymans 8

'Observer, The' 11
Olantigh Towers 68
Otford Palace 14
Otford Court 68
Oxnead Hall, Norfolk 17
Oxonhoath 4, 8, 9, 24, 38-39, 43, 56, 68
Owl House 68

Pains Hill 58
Palladio, A 28
Palladian villa 25, 28, 29, 48
Parkinson, John 5
parterre 22, 25, 37, 39
Paxton, Sir Joseph 41
Pearson, Frank L 48
Pegwell Bay 42
Penshurst Place 3, 5, 8, 9, 14, 16, 18-19, 21, 24, 40, 56, 68
Pepys 5
Pilton, Messrs. 35
Port Lympne 9, 10, 11, 48, 49, 69
Poussin, Nicholas 25
Powell-Cotton 42, 58
Pulhamite rock 6, 41, 42
Pympne Manor 8, 45, 52, 69

Quex Park 5, 7, 42, 43, 58, 61, 69

Ramsgate 42
Redleaf 8, 36, 41, 69
Repton, Humphry 4, 8, 30, 33, 34, 35
Rhododendrons 8, 40, 53
R.H.S.gardens, Kensington 4
Richmond, Mr 32
Riverhill House 8, 69
Robinson, William 4, 40, 41, 50
Robson, John 7, 10, 42, 43
Rochester 4, 6, 11, 14, 20
Rome 16
Rotunda, La 28
Roydon Hall 3, 16, 20, 69

Saint Augustine's Abbey 10, 12-13
Saint John's Jerusalem 9, 70
Salomon's House 7
Salutation 69
Sackville-West, V 11, 50
Sandling Park 41, 69
Sassoon, Sir P 48
Sandys, Sir Ed. 20
Salvin, Anthony 37, 40

Sayes Court 10
sculpture (and statuary) 3, 15, 16, 17, 21, 22, 24, 36, 38, 48, 61
Scotney Castle 8, 9, 40, 41, 70
Sevenoaks 35
Sissinghurst Castle 45, 50, 54-55, 69
Sydney, Sir P 16
Somerhill 40, 70
South America 53
South Park, Penshurst 40
Southborough 7
S.P.A.B. 56
Squerryes Court 3, 9, 10, 20, 23, 25, 26-27, 28, 58, 62, 70
Speed family 57
Stanhope, Earl of 5
Stone, Nicholas 17
Stoneacre, Otham 4, 45
Stonepitts 47
Stonewall Park 70
Stour Valley 10, 32
Sundridge Park 33
Swaylands 8 40, 41, 70
Tennant, H.J. 47
Terrace gardens 3, 13, 16, 18, 19, 20, 22, 24, 25, 26, 27, 34, 35, 36, 40, 45, 47, 48, 56
Tilden, P 11, 48
Tompsett, B 53
Triggs, Inigo 47
Tradescant J.sen. & jun. 5, 10, 16, 17
Tunbridge Wells 8, 35, 42, 57
Tunbridge High Rocks Park 8

United States of America 5, 6

Valence 32, 70
Versailles 3, 5, 22, 25
villa garden 4, 8, 35, 36
Vinters Park 33, 70

Wakehurst Place 8, 41
Waldershare park 24, 25, 29, 70
Walmer Castle 70
Weald 7, 8, 9, 37, 40, 41
Wellard, J 52
Wells, H.G. 8, 36
Wells, W. 36
Weaver, Lawrence 45
Westbury Court 25
West Farleigh 25
West Indies 5
Wharton, Edith 48
Whistler, R 48
White House, Wrotham 47
William and Mary 25
wilderness 15, 21, 24, 25, 29, 58
Wilson, E.H. 6
Winchester Castle 15, 58
Winchelsea, Lord 16
Wise, Henry 25
Wittersham House 47
Wood, J.G. 14
Wordsworth, William 41
Wotton, Lord 10
Wright T. 58
Wyatt, James 30, 32, 35
Wyatt, Samuel 63